POLITICAL ECONOMY: PAST AND PRESENT

A Review of Leading Theories of Economic Policy

Political Economy:
Past and Present

A REVIEW OF LEADING THEORIES
OF ECONOMIC POLICY

LORD ROBBINS

New York   Columbia University Press   1976

Published in Great Britain in 1976 by The Macmillan Press Ltd.

Library of Congress Catalog Card Number: 76-7264
ISBN: 0-231-04128-4
Printed in Great Britain

95866

Contents

Preface

The genesis of this book was as follows. In the spring of 1974, my friends at the University of Cape Town invited me to lecture there in the Economics Faculty and indicated the History of Economic Thought or Problems of Contemporary Economic Policy as appropriate subjects.

Now, in the past, I had already written several works on the history of economic thought, in most of which I had tried explicitly to present the subjects of my enquiries without committing myself to final evaluation of their logical validity or their bearing on practice. I had also written a good many papers and lectures on contemporary economic policy. It was therefore not unnatural that it should have occurred to me that, from my point of view, it would be congenial to combine the two areas and to say, in a more or less systematic way, what I thought of earlier views and their relevance in contemporary applications. In the concluding section of my *Theory of Economic Policy in English Classical Political Economy*, written some twenty years ago, I had expressed just such an aspiration. Having presented the Classical theories in this respect, I wrote,

How interesting it would be . . . to proceed to examine to what extent, according to our lights and our ethical postulates, these contributions are in any sense valid. To what extent is their theory of the market sustained by the results of more recent analysis? How far were they justified in the hope that financial controls (about the exact nature of which they never reached agreement) were sufficient to maintain the stability of the envelope of aggregate demand which the System of Economic Freedom postulated? Did their theory of property overlook overriding technical influences tending to general monopoly? In what measure has this theory been rendered obsolete by the development of joint-stock companies and the limited-liability principle? How do our present views regarding population tendencies affect our conception of the limits of the eleemosynary function? Were the Classical Economists right in their apprehensions of over-all collectivism?

My tolerant hosts concurred with my suggestion that I should attempt just that. My lectures therefore followed such a plan.

These chapters are based upon what I said in that course. Those who did me the honour of attendance may recognise some of the language and the general sequence of argument; nothing in this final recension in any way diverges from its implicit background of thought. But, in writing up my notes, I have found it necessary to expand so much in regard to certain topics to which I could then only find time to make brief allusion that my book is more than twice as long as the original lectures.

In following my plan, since I did not wish to deal at any length with matters I had investigated elsewhere in some detail, my treatment of the historical material conforms more to the model of the composite ideal-type rather than to that of the copious compilation of actual quotations which was the basis of my earlier work in this field. In contrast to that, this is a critique, a reconstruction rather than a history. From time to time where the nature of the subject matter made it seem inevitable, there appears material which I have used elsewhere. But I have tried to keep such citations to a minimum. I hope therefore that those who have read my earlier books will not find too much repetition; while those who have not will be able to follow my argument without any strong compulsion to look elsewhere – although naturally I should be flattered were they to do so.

I trust that my sub-title – *A Review of Leading Theories of Economic Policy* – indicates sufficiently both my intentions and the limitations of what I have tried to do. The sequence of chapter headings and their sections follows what aspires to be a more or less logical structure; but the contents are essentially a series of appraisals and suggestions rather than a comprehensive treatise. I attempt to rough out a perspective rather than to paint a complete picture, still less to present detailed plans or appraisals of contemporary policies. In the last analysis, I suppose, my motive in writing is to make definite statements of my own views on the subjects dealt with, rather than leave them to be inferred from casual asides in my various works on the history of thought approaching their subjects from what was intended to be a more detached standpoint.

I should like to take this opportunity of thanking once more the members of the Economics Faculty at Cape Town for all that they did during the weeks in which my wife and I enjoyed their warm hospitality.

London School of Economics
September 1975

CHAPTER 1

Introduction and Plan

POLITICAL ECONOMY AS A TITLE AND AS A SUBJECT

The term 'Political Economy', which I have chosen as the main part of the title of this book, has two alternative meanings. In the beginning, as in Sir James Steuart's *Principles of Political Economy* or Adam Smith's *Wealth of Nations*, it covered the entire universe of discourse of economic science and the theory of economic policy. Thus, while the first three books of Adam Smith's great work are devoted to the analysis of the market economy and its progress through history, the fourth and fifth are directed to alternative systems of policy and the principles of public finance: and this latter matter was explicitly recognised as being part of the subject. 'Political Economy', says the introduction to book IV, 'considered as a branch of the science of a statesman or legislator proposes two distinct objects: first to provide a plentiful revenue or subsistence for the people, or more properly to enable them to provide such a revenue or subsistence for themselves; and, secondly, to supply the state or commonwealth with a revenue sufficient for the public services. It proposes to enrich both the people and the sovereign.' So that Political Economy, in the sense of the contents of Smith's book, not only described how the economic system actually worked, or could work, but also how, according to the assumptions of the author, it ought to be made, or allowed, to work. This usage was followed in general by the majority of Classical Economists. Thus description and prescription enjoyed a common title.*

*The title of Mill's famous treatise, *Principles of Political Economy with some of their Applications to Social Philosophy*, shows increasing sophistication in this respect.

In recent years, however, it has become customary to drop the adjective 'political' and to use the term 'Economics' to designate the analysis and description of economic phenomena and to regard the discussion of what is desirable in the way of policy as a distinct, though related, speculative area. This has a double advantage. It recognises the ranges of both individual and collective behaviour which, in some way or other, are influenced by the scarcity of resources in relation to objectives; at the same time it removes, or should remove, any presumption that generalisations about such behaviour have *in themselves* any normative presumption. Adam Smith's description of the 'political economy considered as the science of a statesman or legislator', quoted above, clearly included all sorts of assertions relating to social and political values, which nowadays would be recognised as having a logical status completely different from assertions of how economic behaviour takes place or how it could take place in various assumed conditions. A terminology which reminds us of this is, or should be, a help to clear thinking – though it must be admitted that there are still some who are apparently congenitally incapable of seeing the difference.

At the same time, the dropping of the wider coverage of the label enables us to use it in a sense which is much less misleading. Economics, as a positive science, has no status as ethical or political prescription. But no one in his senses would contend that it is reasonable to prescribe what is desirable in this respect without knowledge of what is possible – of what effects are likely to follow from what specific types of individual or political action – any more than it would be reasonable to proceed to architectural design without prior knowledge of materials and their potentialities. It is therefore only natural but also highly to be recommended that, with due recognition of the differences, discussion of the problems of what is practically desirable in this field should be conducted against a background of relevant scientific knowledge; and it is a fortunate circumstance that the change in terminological habits described above should have left the term 'Political Economy' free for use in this connection.

That, at any rate, is the significance of my use of this term in the title of this book. Political Economy in my vocabulary is not scientific economics, a collection of value-free generalisations about the way in which economic systems work. It is a discussion of principles of public policy in the economic field: and while it makes appeal to the findings of economic science, it also involves assumptions which, in the nature of things, lie outside positive science and which are essentially normative in character. It consists of prescription rather than description; although, since it is concerned with practice, its recommendations make use of what aspires to be a scientific examination of the results of action rather than wishful thinking regardless of consequences.*

THE HISTORICAL SETTING

Political Economy thus conceived is essentially a search for solutions to problems of policy. And since in this respect neither the enquiring mind nor the problems with which it seeks to grapple start from a *tabula rasa*, it follows that any discussion must take some account of previous opinions and past experiences. The treatment need not be historical in the sense that the precise origins of the opinions under discussion must be traced in detail or, for that matter, their exact relation to the historical circumstances amid which they arose. But because contemporary thought is the inheritor of the speculations of the

---

*It may be asked what is the connection between *Political Economy* thus conceived and the so-called *Welfare Economics* which has been so fashionable in the last half century. The answer is that it adopts overt judgements and procedures which are often merely implicit in discussions under this later heading and goes beyond them in many ways. Thus the earlier *Welfare Economics* continually invoked interpersonal comparisons involving the assumption of equality of capacity for satisfaction which, however justifiable as ethical assumptions, are clearly not demonstrable either by observation or introspection. Later on, awareness of this fact has driven more sensitive and cautious practitioners to a restriction of claims for *scientific* status to propositions appearing to invoke only comparisons with the so-called Pareto optimum. But these, too, if they approach within a thousand miles of practical application, usually prove to involve concealed neglect of considerations involving judgements of value. I would be the last to deny the importance of the distinction between purely scientific economic analysis and normative prescription. But, for me at any rate, *Welfare Economics* has always seemed a very draughty half-way house. Why not cross the dividing line and, like the Classical Economists before us, when we pass to prescription, use, with due acknowledgement – which they did not always make – whatever ethical and political premises seem appropriate? I have examined this problem at greater length in my *Politics and Economics* (London: Macmillan, 1963) pp. 3-26.

past, a certain scheme of historical reference gives substance both by way of continuity and of contrast to any examination of present perplexities. The present enterprise will therefore proceed by some review of past theories and appraisal of their present applications.

Now, of course, there has been discussion of problems of Political Economy in this sense almost since the beginning of history. But, until a comparatively recent date, the characteristic of such discussion has been that it was predominantly *ad hoc*, either in the examination of the tendencies of particular policies or in the appraisal of particular problems of moral or political action. The immense pamphlet literature of the so-called Mercantilist period was predominantly conceived with special problems of regulation of trade, coinage, poor relief and so on; while the references to economic problems of Greek Philosophy, the Scholastic theologians and some of the early modern lawyers were directed principally to isolated problems which, if they had a more generalised basis, were yet to be conceived against a background of public or private morality rather than any systematic view of the economic problems of society as a whole. It is not until the emergence in the eighteenth century of analysis of economic phenomena as an interconnected whole – *Economics* in the modern sense – in the works of the Physiocrats and the Scotish Philosophers and their followers that we find the norms and prescriptions relating to economic policy – that is to say, *Political Economy*, in my sense of the word – acquiring also the appearance of a system;* and in spite of the transitory blaze of popularity in French and Continental court circles of the former group, it is the thought of the latter whose work in this respect still influences, by way of attraction or repulsion, the thought of our present age.

Hence, in what follows, although there will be occasional references to earlier thought on these matters, the main focus of reference and criticism will be to what may be called Classical Political Economy and, within this broad category, particularly to the prescriptions of the British Classical Economists. In

---

*I do not list here the remarkable *Essai sur le Commerce* of Cantillon since this was almost entirely pure economics in the modern sense of the word, and which, in its celebrated discussion of population, explicitly repudiated evaluation.

certain contexts, however, where wide ideological tendencies occupy the centre of the stage, I shall not deny myself looser references to what I shall call Classical Liberalism.

There is a further reason for this focus. Contemporary thought on matters of Political Economy often tends in directions which involve, in the end, either complete Collectivism or complete Anarchy, total coercion or general conflict. Neither of these tendencies seems to me to be compatible with the idea of a society which is both free and orderly. Now it was the virtue of the Classical System that it offered an alternative which rejected both; and although, in all sorts of ways, we have discovered some of the Classical conceptions to be incomplete or erroneous, it still seems worthwhile examining to what extent these deficiencies are due to fundamental misconception or only to inadequate coverage of the field. As will be seen from the development of the argument, my own belief is that both kinds of deficiency are involved. But I still hold that amendments are possible which afford the possibility of avoiding the appalling horrors of either of the extreme tendencies I have mentioned. It is indeed in that hope that these chapters have been written.

THE ESSENCE OF THE CLASSICAL SYSTEM

Let me begin, therefore, by roughing out the main outlines of the Classical System in this respect.

The major analytical background to Classical Political Economy was Adam Smith's exposition of the way in which the division of labour was governed by the influence of the market. Needless to say, recognition of the place of the division of labour in the social bond was not a new discovery. Some reference to it is as old as the famous conversation between Socrates and Glaucon in Plato's *Republic* about the City of the Pigs; and a somewhat mechanical rehearsal of its advantages can be traced in a great deal of rather boring literature between that and the *Wealth of Nations*. But it was Adam Smith who brought them to life, so to speak, by his vivid exposition. Who can forget the concluding paragraph of chapter I book I with its demonstration of the world-wide extent of the spontaneous co-operation which brought it about that 'the accommodation

5

of an European prince not always so much exceeds that of an industrious and frugal peasant, as the accommodation of the latter exceeds that of many an African king, the absolute master of the lives and liberties of ten thousand naked savages'?* It was Adam Smith, too, who, after showing the advantages of the division of labour, attempted to show too how, given a reasonable setting of law and order, it was controlled and guided by the market acting through the incentives which it provided to the private interests of the individual producers or small groups of such persons. Classical Economics contains much more intricate and detailed analysis than this. But it is to get the whole perspective wrong not to put it in the centre of the picture.

It is not difficult to see how such a conception of order arising from spontaneous exchange relationships should have harmonised with the general presumptions regarding the importance of civil and intellectual liberty which were developing during this period. If the ethical objective was the greatest happiness, why should it not be assumed that at least, so far as individual enjoyments were concerned, the adult person was not better able to judge for himself than others? It would be a mistake to assume that all those who shared these sentiments in principle would have subscribed to the detailed arguments of John Stuart Mill's classic essay *On Liberty*. But that 'the System of Natural Liberty', as Adam Smith called it, evoked strong ethical sympathies among the leading economists of that period is incontestable. Thus liberty in the field of individual choice and liberty in the organisation of production became the innovating doctrines of Classical Political Economy.

Having said this, however, it is desirable immediately to make it clear that liberty as conceived by these thinkers did not exclude the conception of order. It was not a liberty to do just anything. At all times there was involved the assumption of a framework of law which derived its *raison d'être* from the necessity of preventing the freedom of any one person or group of persons interfering with the liberty of others. Classical Liberalism therefore is to be sharply distinguished from philosophical anarchism, according to which, if all coercive laws

---

Wealth of Nations, ed. E. Cannan (1896) vol. I, p. 14.

and institutions supported by law were removed, a natural harmony would be established. Godwin, whose *Enquiry Concerning Political Justice* is to be regarded as the *locus classicus* of that point of view, actually argued that if only law and property were abolished, all social evils would vanish and the race might even become immortal. This would have been rejected by any Classical Economist, as would have been his quaint suggestion that, in similar circumstances what Malthus called 'the passion between the sexes' would diminish.* They certainly believed that, within an appropriate framework of law, spontaneous relations would themselves give rise to what, perhaps misleadingly, Adam Smith had described as a 'natural order'. But, for them, the existence of a state with an apparatus of coercion was an essential prerequisite of any conception of social liberty and was in the same sense 'natural' if confined to its proper limitations. It may well be that, in their opposition to the restrictive systems of the past, the Classical writers occasionally used language which may have highlighted the claims and utility of freedom and may have seemed to underestimate the essential restraints of law and the positive functions of the state. But the identification of the liberty envisaged by the liberal tradition with the absence of a coercive framework, so frequent among the ignorant or the politically interested, is completely without foundation. The Liberal prescriptions assumed throughout an apparatus of law and order.

Thus to get a proper historical perspective, it is important to note that in the closest juxtaposition with Smith's own recommendation of the 'System of Natural Liberty' was his enumeration of the necessary powers of the sovereign which, beside the duty of maintaining defence and devising and enforcing internal law, included the duty of providing public works and institutions which, to use his own words, 'can never be for the interest of any individual, or small number of individuals, to

---

*It is amusing to recall the comment of Malthus on the suggestion 'A writer may tell me that he thinks man will ultimately become an ostrich. I cannot properly contradict him. But before he can expect to bring any reasonable person over to his opinion, he ought to show that the necks of mankind have been gradually elongating; that the lips have grown harder and more prominent; that the legs and feet are daily altering their shape; and that the hair is beginning to change into stubs of feathers. And till the probability of so wonderful a conversion can be shown, it is surely lost time and energy to expatiate on the happiness of such a state.' *Essay on the Principle of Population,* 1st edn (1798) p. 45.

erect and maintain: because the profit can never repay the expense to any individual or small number of individuals though it may frequently do much more than repay it to a great society'.* Indeed it is worthwhile emphasising the fact, too often neglected by popular historians of economic ideas, that the Classical outlook in contrast with that of earlier ages was positively in favour of the assumption by the state of some functions previously assumed by private enterprise, the collection of taxes, the control of turnpikes, the manufacture of certain forms of money, not to mention the abolition of private mercenary armies. Moreover, as can be shown in detail, many of them were pioneers in urging state activity in the provision of important welfare services, education, relief of certain types of poverty and so on.†

But if this was so, how then are we to distinguish this outlook from other social philosophies which postulate order and an apparatus of coercion? The answer is simple. Whereas the other systems in question, Classical Conservatism for example, regard order as an end in itself – something having ethical and aesthetic intrinsic desirability, the Classical Liberal outlook regards it as a means – a means of preserving liberty, a means therefore whose use is to be kept at a minimum necessary for the discharge of that function.‡ In Plato's *Republic*, for instance, the order there aimed at is an order which is represented as an ultimate good in itself, an emblem of justice in its ultimate acceptance, whereas the legal order of Classical Liberalism is simply an apparatus designed to secure that one man's liberty of action does not impede the liberty of action of his fellows. It is something which is required in order that liberty should be achieved. It is this which provided a clear basis for evaluation. If the objective of law was to create the conditions of freedom then the criteria were unmistakable. A good law increased the *area* of happiness and freedom; a bad law diminished it. Thus it was not the absolute extent of the law which was to be judged desirable or undesirable; it was the extent to which it facilitated harmonious liberty.

---

*Wealth of Nations, vol. ii, p. 209.

†See my *Theory of Economic Policy in English Classical Political Economy* (London: Macmillan, 1952) chs 1–3.

‡See my lecture 'Freedom and Order', in my *Politics and Economics*, pp. 27–52.

There is, moreover, a further contrast. The authoritarian systems, both ancient and modern, tend to assume that there will be no order anywhere unless it is enforced from above, no acceptable activity, at least in the economic sphere, unless controlled by central authority. In contrast, as we have seen, the essence of Classical Liberalism was the belief that, within a suitable system of general rules and institutions, there will arise spontaneous relationships also deserving the term 'order' but which are self-sustaining and, within the limits prescribed by the rules, need no detailed and specific regulation.* Such an outlook would have been very unwise if it had argued that in *no* circumstances would direct regulation of this sort be desirable – and unwisdom of this sort can sometimes be discovered among camp followers and extremists. But that it should be the exception rather than the rule was a distinguishing feature of the central position.

PLAN OF THE FOLLOWING CHAPTERS

Described in these very general terms it might appear that there was little in general conception in the outlook of Classical Political Economists which differed from the outlook of those with similar ideals in our own day. In an earlier work, already cited,† I have drawn attention to the virtual identity of the conceptions involved in Adam Smith's description of the functions of the sovereign quoted above‡ and the formulation in John Maynard Keynes's famous tract *The End of Laissez Faire* which runs as follows: 'The most important Agenda of the state relate not to those activities which private individuals are already fulfilling but to those functions which fall outside the sphere of the individual, to those decisions which are made by *no one* if the state does not make them. The important thing for government is not to do things which individuals are doing already and to do them a little better or a little worse: but to do those things which are not done at all.'§

*For a powerful development of this point of view see Professor F. A. Hayek's *Law, Legislation and Liberty* (Chicago University Press, 1973) vol. I.
† *Theory of Economic Policy in English Classical Political Economy*, p. 37.
‡pp. 7–8.
§*Collected Writings of John Maynard Keynes* (London: Macmillan, 1972) vol. IX, p. 291.

Thus there is at least formal, and I should also say, spiritual continuity in what may be called the Liberal outlook in this respect – and by Liberal I mean not (repeat *not*) what is meant by that word nowadays in the United States, or indeed in the United Kingdom, in the party sense, but rather the general outlook springing from the great eighteenth- and nineteenth-century social philosophers, David Hume, Adam Smith, Tocqueville, John Stuart Mill, Henry Sidgwick and others. But, as time goes on, although the *prime desiderata* remain unchanged, the environment of opportunity and proximate objectives alters. Technique changes, the quantity and quality of the population change, as does the irrational deposit of past history. Individual values change and so too do some social goals. And, with all such changes, there emerge new problems, new centres of interest for Political Economy, new prescriptions to be formulated. It is an amusing circumstance that Keynes who, in the mood in which he wrote the passage I have quoted, certainly thought that he was effecting something of a break with the Classical tradition should – unconsciously no doubt – have used a formula so exactly parallel with Adam Smith's. But there can be no question that the substantial focus of his attention was different. The twentieth-century problems which seemed to him of paramount importance were not the same as those which seemed important to Adam Smith.

In fact I suspect that there was much more in common between Keynes and his predecessors than at that time he would have been willing to admit; and I, personally, am very positively conscious of the continuity of the Liberal tradition, not only in its most general formulation but also in some at least of its particular recommendations. Nevertheless there are differences, both in the concrete problems which present themselves and also in some of the modes of approaching their solution. That indeed is the justification I would plead in presenting this review.

The general plan is as follows. The next chapter will discuss the Political Economy of Consumption. Two chapters will then be devoted to an exposition and critique of the Classical theory of free enterprise in the Organisation of Production. These will be followed by two chapters examining assumptions and policies regarding the Stability of the System as a Whole; and these in turn by two chapters on Welfare and Distribution. A chapter will then be devoted to a discussion of Collectivism, and Syndicalism, and the more detailed analysis will be rounded off by a chapter on International Economic Relations. A concluding chapter will discuss the relations between Politics and Political Economy.

CHAPTER 2

The Political Economy of Consumption

COLLECTIVE GOODS AND SERVICES

In considering the flow of goods and services which constitute the consumption of the citizens it is important to take account of the very considerable proportion of that flow, which even in a Liberal economy is determined by collective decision.

These fall into two groups; first those such as defence, the availability of roads, the arrangements for disposal of sewage, the provision of parks and such like amenities which afford what, in the jargon of the Theory of Public Finance, is called indiscriminate benefit, in that, for technical or institutional reasons, their use or service is not confined to particular individuals; secondly certain services which, although available to all citizens or to groups of citizens, are individually enjoyed and the benefit of which can therefore be regarded as at least in part discriminate – education, medical care, the relief of poverty and so on.

Now the common characteristic of these two groups is *not* that they are provided by collective *organisations* but that their availability and volume is the result of collective *decision*. It is quite easy to find cases where all the assembling and constructive work on the scarce resources involved is performed by private enterprise. But the choice of how much defence to afford, of where, and of what degree of durability, roads are to be constructed, or how much free education or free hospital service is to be provided, is essentially public. How exactly it is expressed is clearly a matter which varies with political constitutions. It may be made by messianic leaders, by self-perpetuating totalitarian party executives or by the numerous variants of elected governmental assemblies. But whether it is made for the public by authoritarian groups or by bodies representative of a majority in societies which profess in some degree democratic ideals, its effects are radically different from the effects of individual choices in the non-collectivist area of consumption.

Take, for instance, defence: in most Western communities there are some people who, rightly or wrongly, think they need no defence at all and that all defence expenditure is wasteful. At the other end of the spectrum of opinion, let us hope a wider band, there are people who think that the Western communities do not provide sufficiently for defence and are in danger of being overrun, like the Roman Empire, by barbarians. But whatever decision is taken, it applies collectively: the individuals concerned have to put up with the choice of the government. The same applies to all the other services falling into this classification. An individual voter may not want so much provision of, say, motor roads or free education. But once the decision is taken he has to take – or refrain from taking – what is available until he can find sufficient supporters to get the government to change its policy.

Both the objectives and the organisation of this kind of choice are thus *political* in a much more direct sense than individual choice involving discriminate benefit. It is true that, since the provision of the services in question involves the use of scarce resources, there is an economic aspect to the decisions involved, and the direct costs at least are certainly capable of quantification. But what of the enjoyments? There may be some cases, such as road construction, in which, by making arbitrary assumptions concerning the value of the time saved and the direct amenity produced, some conventional valuation may be calculated. This is the *raison d'être* of the fashionable cost-benefit analysis whose utility in certain restricted fields it would be a mistake to decry. But, in any full perspective, the limitations are obvious. Even so far as road construction is concerned, this kind of analysis is not the last word: it may be completely overshadowed by wider considerations of lay-out and general amenity. Again, who is to quantify, in any precise sense, the benefits involved in various alternatives of free education?

These are matters of direct political valuations, as indeed are the related questions relating to alternative political organisations for making them. How should the responsible bodies be constituted – by majority vote, by proportional representation, by *ad hoc* appointment? Or should some be the subject of specific referenda? These are questions relating to what Adam Smith called the 'science of the statesman',* rather than the usual concerns of the Political Economist: But they are the background of much that he has to say and it is highly desirable that he should be aware of his own attitude to the answers under the present heading of discussion. There are, of course, quite major questions of the desirable extent of collective choice in those fields where it is not technically inevitable – the cases where, although the choice is collective, the benefit is to some extent at any rate discriminate and where therefore choice could be individual – questions involving incentives both to work and to save; and these may be regarded as central among the problems of Political Economy. But they are better dealt with at a later stage when we are discussing distribution and welfare.

THE IDEOLOGY OF INDIVIDUAL CHOICE

Where the great field of discriminate benefit was concerned there can be no doubt of the attitude of the Classical Economists. They believed in freedom of choice on the part of mature adult individuals. They would certainly not have extended this conception to non-adults although doubtless, as between regimes of strict discipline imposed for their own sake and regimes designed to train for eventual liberty they would have been unanimous in choosing the latter. But, having regard to the manifold differences of taste and inclination, where mature persons were concerned they would have regarded it as a departure from the ideal if the state were to impose any but very exceptional limitations on personal conduct in this respect. This assumption, I am sure, would have been general. 'Generally speaking' said Bentham, 'there is no one who knows what is for

---

* *Wealth of Nations*, vol. 1, p. 395. In another place he contrasted this science with 'the skill of that insidious and crafty animal vulgarity called a statesman or politician' (p. 432).

your interest so well as yourself – no one who is disposed with so much ardour and constancy to pursue it';* and J. B. Say, speaking for a wider tradition, laid it down that 'Chaque homme en particulier est seul capable d'apprecier avec justice la perte et l'avantage qui result pour lui ou pour sa famille, de chacune de ses consommations, puisque cette perte et cet avantage sont relatifs à sa fortune, au rang qu'il occupe dans la société, à ces besoins, à ceux de sa famille, et même à ses goûts personnels.'†

Let me say at once that I believe strictly in this prescription. For me it is a fundamental essential of a morally acceptable mature society.‡ A state of affairs in which priests or monarchs or officials prescribe what grown-up men and women shall do in their capacity as consumers where such actions have no deleterious indirect effects, seems to be the negation of civilisation as I think it ought to be, even though I am not unaware that there have been many civilisations of the past, not all of whose manifestations are to be condemned, where such conditions did not prevail. But if we consider modern times and pay some attention to conditions in the Communist section of the world where you cannot buy a newspaper or book from the West if it has not the right ideological complexion and where writers and scientists who try to publish dissident views are deported or sent to bogus psychiatric asylums, the proof of the pudding seems to be unmistakable. Freedom in the sphere of this kind of private consumption is not everything. But it is one of the essential constituents of the good society.

CAVEAT EMPTOR AND ADVERTISEMENT

Nevertheless in the complexity of modern life this is by no means all that is to be said about consumption in a free society. Thus, to begin with the simplest case, in order that the customer may get what he wants, he must know in a broad way what he is getting; and there are many ways in which the maxim *caveat*

---

*Jeremy Bentham, 'Manual of Political Economy', *Works,* ed. Bowring (1838–43) vol. III, p. 33.
†*Traité D'Economie Politique,* 3rd edn (Paris, 1817) vol. II, p.214.
‡See a more extensive discussion of this conception below, Chapter 11, pp. 173–6.

emptor – let the buyer beware – admirable though it may be as a safeguard against fussy regulation, is not enough.

The Classical Economists did not pay as much attention to this problem as we do. There is an interesting passage in Ricardo's *Proposals for an Economical and Secure Currency* in which he endorses Say's contention that interference of government is justifiable to prevent fraud and to certify facts.

> In the examinations to which medical practitioners are obliged to submit, there is no improper interference: for it is necessary to the welfare of the people, that the fact of their having acquired a certain portion of knowledge respecting the diseases of the human frame should be ascertained and certified. The same may be said of the stamp which the government puts on plate and money: it thereby prevents fraud and saves the necessity of having recourse on each purchase and sale to a difficult chemical process.*

Furthermore, John Stuart Mill in his chapter on the 'Grounds and Limits of the *Laissez Faire* Principle' says that 'the proposition that the consumer is a competent judge of the commodity, can be admitted only with numerous abatements and exceptions'; but he does not follow this up in any detail, preferring to dilate on certain problems of education which will be germane to the argument of this survey at a later stage. On the whole the attention of Classical Political Economy was more directed to the possibility of the abuse of certification in the interest of special groups, as in Adam Smith's well-known denunciation of the apprenticeship regulations of corporations, than to the desirability of protection in this way. In those days there was probably much justification for such a balance of emphasis; and even nowadays the abuses of closed associations of producers requiring unnecessarily long periods of training and preposterous discrimination against women are still conspicuous and still deserve continuous vigilance and exposure. But in our age, with the vastly greater technical complication of goods and services, the negative emphasis is not enough. We must never forget the perpetual pressure for privileges which are not technically necessary and should be on guard against it. But the proper information of the consumer concerning the quality and poten-

Works, ed. P. Sraffa (Cambridge University Press, 1951) vol. IV, p.73.

tialities of what he is buying is something which, in a large range of cases, needs positive enforcement by law.

It is from this point of view that we may take some note of the problems of advertising. I know few subjects on which more nonsense is talked than this. *Soi-disant* sociological and economic experts elaborate a picture of a world in which the whole area of consumer demand is manipulated at will by the manufacturers of shoddy and inimical products. The controlling power of demand is alleged to be a fiction. The consumer is a passive medium whose response is conditioned entirely by the active propaganda of the producer. And all this is claimed as the most startling discovery, an amazing breakthrough of the 'New Economics' rendering obsolete all earlier analysis.

In fact this is largely erroneous. Advertisement in the narrow sense of the word is simply a leading species of the much larger genus, information combined with persuasion: and the belief is puerile that because some advertisement is fraudulent and some methods not to our taste, advertisement in general can be thought out of any complex society. So too is the exaggerated view of its role in shaping consumer (or producer) demand already mentioned. It is perfectly true that properly managed advertisement helps to sell a product by bringing its existence to the notice of potential buyers. It is also true that, persuasively argued, it may tempt some to buy who would not have done so had there been no overtone of appeal to herd instinct, snobbery and/or general desire for comfort and happiness. But it is not true that it can often succeed for very long if the object advertised does not fulfil its promises. The idea that most buyers of advertised goods are incapable of judging what does and what does not fulfil the object of purchase rests upon too poor a view of the perceptive apparatus of the average man or woman. As for the business of creating demand for products which do not eventually fit the needs or the tastes of the moment, any one who has had experience of such attempts must be provoked to a certain degree of wry mirth at the alleged ease of such a process. It is a facility more prevalent in the imagination of second-rate literary men than in the world of practical business.

Nevertheless the consumer does need some protection in this respect. The idea that lines can easily be drawn between information and persuasion which are administratively practical, or even socially desirable, is unrealistic. What is the moral difference between the cry 'flowers for sale' and 'buy my violets, pretty lady'? What is important is that, in so far as ignorance in consumption may lead to results which the buyer himself would regard as deleterious – as with poisons – or other than those expected – as with many health aids and some financial promises – he should be so informed; and it is important that false claims should be prohibited. From the libertarian point of view, it is not a matter for direct public prohibition that some people should be persuaded by ingenious talk or pictures to buy goods or services which other people regard as frivolous or vulgar, though it may well be hoped that education will increase fastidiousness in this respect. But it is important that they should know physically damaging consequences which may be associated with certain purchases and be protected from claims whch are technically inadmissible. Such protection may be very difficult to adminster sensibly. The very statement seems to open the door to all sorts of officious requirements and prohibitions. But I see no escape from the general principle: and its importance, especially in connection with advertisement relating to health, seems to me incontestable.

THE EXTERNAL DISECONOMIES OF CONSUMPTION

As I have said, there are indications in the works of the Classical Economists that such qualifications of the principle of *caveat emptor* would not have surprised them. More remote from their field of vision, although not necessarily antipathetic to it, were limitations on freedom of choice in consumption which may be involved as a result of certain indirect effects not taken into account by the market mechanism. By this I do not have in mind the effects of fashion or what moralists might call bad example: I mean something much more tangible than that, namely the objective changes in the position of groups due to the indirect effects of the consumption of individuals – what, in a terminology derived by extension from Marshall's theory of production with its internal and external economies, are called the external diseconomies of consumption. Simple examples are the pollution of the atmosphere by a substantial population of private cars or the noise engendered in the vicinity of airports.

It is doubtful whether there is anything very controversial about the need to limit such diseconomies, any more than there is regarding the need to limit the similar diseconomies of production, factory smoke or poisonous effluents in public waters. Some of these are already controlled by law, others are likely to become so. There are indeed very difficult problems of administration here. But there are no reasonable differences of opinion regarding the principle; and I see no reason at all to suppose opposition by earlier economists in the Classical tradition, although there may have been a handful of otherwise reputable thinkers who had blind spots in this connection.

But there are wider aspects of the same problem which are perhaps more controversial. They concern changes in the physical environment which may follow complete freedom in the commissioning of accommodation and the lay-out of the environment. And since much capital is often made of the alleged neglect of this problem – by those who never read anything written the day before yesterday – perhaps I may be permitted to quote a passage which I myself wrote some quarter of a century ago when concern with discussion of this sort commanded much less public support.

Here is a pleasant hillside [I said]. If you pay, you can procure a plot and induce a builder to erect for you an agreeable dwelling. What could be more delightful? But if, at the same time, other consumers are moved by the same impulse, the result is insensibly changed. The total picture, which affects your enjoyment and theirs, never comes into the market; and the end product may easily be something in which the quality of enjoyment is substantially lower than might easily have been the case if collective forethought had paid some attention, not so much to the design of the buildings – I have some suspicions of official architects – but at least the lay-out of plots and road facilities. An apparatus of choice which is focussed entirely on discriminate benefit, to the neglect of what is indiscriminate, may thus easily leave out here something which is vitally significant for the texture and tone of daily life. Who can look at the shambles which is Greater London today without acknowledging that with all the increase in private happiness which has come from this proliferation of villadom – and the increase is very real – something quite fundamental has been forgotten.*

Save for the insertion of a positive recognition of the desirability of some control of height, there is nothing in this passage which I would wish to alter today: and I would freely admit that it is a deficiency in nineteenth-century Classicism that the need for collective planning in this connection was not explicitly recognised. One reason for such neglect I suggest is fairly obvious. In the heyday of the Classical system the lay-out of capital cities at least was still in the hands of great landowners who did in fact plan their properties as a whole: we owe the amenities of the London squares, in so far as they have not been allowed to be ruined – often by public autocracy – to this sort of control. At the same time, although there were developing all sorts of sinks of urban development where there was no such planning, the pressure of population on the amenities of the countryside was not yet oppressive. We should always remember when we speak of the damage to England's green and pleasant land that it is largely twentieth-century developments to meet the demands of a better-off and a much more numerous population that is responsible for the soulless suburbs of outer London and the ruination of much of the Home Counties. How lovely London must have been when Coleridge sat on the brow of Highgate and Ruskin looked southward from Denmark Hill. Apart from John Stuart Mill's well-known plea for the stationary state and its solitudes, I know no evidence which would justify the claim that the Classical Political Economists anticipated this problem.† I hope that they would have agreed that some sort of planning of the development of the physical environment was desirable, though of course it is very easy to think of this being administered with corruption or inefficiency which too often happens today. But that action limiting completely unfettered freedom of choice is justified where indiscriminate negative benefit is involved seems to me clear.

Nevertheless important though this all is, it is also desirable that it should not be carried too far. Again I venture to quote myself of a quarter of a century ago in this connection.

*L. Robbins, *The Economic Problem in Peace and War* (London: Macmillan 1947) pp. 19–20.

†It was of course recognised by Marshall. But he came later on.

It is easy to see how frightfully [this principle] may be abused as a justification for general paternalism. There is scarcely anything which I can do outside the privacy of my home which has not some overtone of indiscriminate benefit or detriment. The clothes I wear, the shows I frequent, the flowers that I plant in my garden, all directly, or through the mysterious influence of fashion, influence the enjoyments and satisfactions of others. Even what is done remote from the perception of others can be conceived to have this aspect. The fact that other people lead a way of life different from my own, that they like and buy pictures and books of which I disapprove and give private banquets of sacred meat and forbidden wines, can clearly be the occasion to some people of most intense mortification. Is this to be included in the calculus of external economies and diseconomies? I can think of few forms of totalitarian regimentation of consumption which could not find some formal justification by appeal to this analysis. It is no accident that the Hegelian philosophers, whose methodical sapping of the intellectual foundations of liberty has been responsible for so many of the evils of our day, always made a bee-line for Mill's useful distinction between self-regarding and other regarding actions, and concentrated all the acid of their anti-libertarian hatred upon dissolving the core of good sense underlying this useful, if not perhaps perfectly phrased, distinction.

Hence I would urge that we must be very watchful. We must not let our distrust of paternalism blind us to the real importance of some special cases which this analysis helps us to understand. But we must be ever on the alert against letting formal analysis without concrete investigation be made the pretext for undervaluing institutions which have an important part to play in the life of a free society. We must realise that too much stress on the penumbra of indiscriminate benefit may easily lead us to ignore the solid core of benefit which is discriminate. And if the exponents of totalitarian methods try to rush us with vague and unproved generalisations about the values of social life as a pattern and the mystic joys of tribal unity, we must be prepared to come back with an insistence that variety and spontaneity are also collective values which the wise man will hesitate to jeopardize.*

*Robbins, *The Economic Problem in Peace and War*, pp.20-2.

CONSUMER SOVEREIGNTY AND THE EDUCATIONAL FUNCTION

Even if effective action were taken both to ensure properly informed choice and to provide safeguards against undesirable side-effects, the libertarian outlook would still encounter criticism on the results of freedom. The so-called state of consumer sovereignty, it is said, has results which are often highly distasteful. Many persons who regard themselves as sensitive – and some who really are – go blue in the face at the folly and the vulgarity of other people's choices, the entertainments they support, the way they spend their spare time and so on and so forth. Thus, in some way or other, not always clearly defined, order, discipline, good taste and high standards in these matters should be enforced by public authority.

I am afraid that, from the libertarian point of view, all this is not acceptable. It is true that the road from serfdom, the rise, owing to increased power to produce, of the hitherto submerged many, has produced many manifestations which I personally find antipathetic – though I do not believe that the consumption patterns of authoritarian ages have always been all that admirable. But if we believe, as I believe and as was, I think, implicit in historical Liberalism, that, necessary though some coercive apparatus may be, only those choices which in some sense are free have ultimate ethical value, then we must be prepared to put up with this. The idea of a world in which free choice leads to no results which we ever disapprove of is obviously a fantastic dream; and at least some of the fuss about other people's alleged deficiencies of taste is itself a sign of spiritual unhealth. The question which has to be faced is whether a world in which choice is unfree is something which we find acceptable; and, if we are that way disposed, since there is plenty of that sort of thing about, I suggest that we look at the unfree systems around us – or, if we are more historically disposed, read up Calvin's Geneva or have a look at Plato's *Laws*.

But this does not mean that the state should do nothing, that the principles of a reasonable liberalism preclude all efforts on the part of government to improve standards of civilisation and

culture. Imagine a world in which there were no manifestations of culture save those showing themselves profitable in the
pecuniary sense, no subsidised art galleries, no institutions of
learning which did not cover all expenses by fees or private
gifts, no parks save those approachable through turnstiles
charging fees which cover all running and overhead expenses,
no public offices which were constructed, save by private
subscription, with any object except to keep out the rain and
other climatic influences inimical to the conduct of business – I
cannot believe that this is a world which any sensible person
would wish to bring into being. Nor, since in greater or lesser
degree at present we actually, as a result of the heritage of the
past, enjoy something considerably better than this, do I think
it at all sensible to let this heritage disappear until members of
the community agree to replace it by payments covering costs
or by purely voluntary subscriptions. I do not believe that any
of the great Classical Economists would have disputed this in
principle, though naturally, as in the case of Adam Smith's
observations about the English universities of his day, they
might have had reservations about particular instances.

If this statement of the case is not convincing or if at least it
appears to be something of an exception to the general philosophy of liberty, I should like to draw attention to the implications of what we may call the Educational Function. There will
be much to be said at a later stage about the functions of the
state in regard to education, both as a supplement to the
institution of the family and as a general medium of communication. But at this point it is sufficient to draw attention to this
function, as it may be discharged by public installations and
institutions designed to keep open the opportunities of the
citizens for access to, and moving amongst, manifestations of
the arts and other civilised general amenities, and for providing
standards of achievement in this respect. In this connection,
from the point of view of the Liberal social philosophy, the
important thing to emphasise is that *the discharge of this function
should not involve monopoly*. It seems to me perfectly legitimate, for
instance, for the state to maintain a radio or television service
if, thereby, it can hope to sustain or spread, for a population of
growing educability, standards of quality and integrity. But
from this same point of view it is *not* legitimate if it seeks to

exclude competition from other sources. Similarly, in regard to learning and the arts, it is perfectly permissible, indeed it is desirable, that the state should subsidise high-grade activities which would otherwise be unprofitable, should maintain museums, academies and chairs in subjects of intrinsic interest but little popular support and sustain examples of high excellence in the performing arts. It is *not* desirable, however, that what is done by way of example and stimulus should be used as an instrument of exclusion, that other such activities should be excluded or subjected to special burdens. It is possible, perhaps, to conceive of future societies most of whose members were so enlightened as to sustain all such activities unsubsidised, without degradation of standards and the dissipation of what has come down to us from earlier times. But it is simply deceiving ourselves to suppose that this is possible in the present age. Therefore if some subsidies to learning and the arts are to be regarded as paternalism, then to that extent I am unashamedly a paternalistic liberal. And I fancy that most of the Classical Economists would have agreed.*

SAVING AND SPENDING

There is a further question which deserves consideration in the context of the Political Economy of Consumption, namely the question of freedom of choice between spending and saving, or, to put it into more abstract terms, the choice between provision for the present and provision for the future.

Now subject to short-period exceptions – of which more in a later chapter – the Classical Economists identified saving with what we should call 'real investment', in physical or in human capital. There are therefore no hesitations in their writings arising from the fact that the acts of saving and investment are distinct operations and that aggregate disturbances may result from a lack of coincidence in plans for such activities. So, since the majority of them believed that accumulation was a good thing, there was no opposition on their part to saving as such.

---

*I know no direct discussion in the Classical Political Economy of questions of this sort. But see John Stuart Mill's remarks on the utility of endowments in his papers on 'Corporation and Church Property, and Endownments', *Collected Works* (Toronto University Press, 1967) vol. IV, pp. 195–222 and vol. V, pp. 613–29.

Malthus, Lauderdale and certain lesser followers were exceptions: they believed that there were at any time upper limits to beneficial accumulation. But for the majority this process made possible by saving was an essential ingredient of economic growth in general; and as the increase of the 'funds destined for the maintenance of labour' combined with the restraint of population increase was their main hope of the increase of wages above subsistence level, they were very much in favour of saving.

They were, moreover, in favour of freedom of choice in this matter. With the exception of John Stuart Mill, they feared the stationary state in which net accumulation had come to a halt; and even Mill's approval of the stationary state rested essentially upon the hope that, in some way or other, population increase had also ceased at a relatively high rate of income per head. They feared even more the declining state in which capital was being consumed either by failure ro renew or by positive destruction. But they did not fear that this would happen *as a result of private decisions*. Indeed with the *Wealth of Nations*, the *locus classicus* of such reflections, immense reliance is placed on just that 'principle which prompts to save . . . the desire of bettering our condition which comes with us from the womb and never leaves us till we go into the grave'; and we find the bald assertion, not perhaps often falsified by history, that 'Great nations are never impoverished by private, though they sometimes are by public prodigality and misconduct'; and later on,

> It is the highest impertinence and presumption . . . in kings and ministers to pretend to watch over the economy of private people and to restrain their expense, either by sumptuary laws, or by prohibiting the importation of foreign luxuries. They are themselves always, and without any exception, the greatest spendthrifts in the society. Let them look well after their own expense, and they may safely trust private people with theirs. If their own extravagance does not ruin the state, that of their subjects never will.*

To the modern eye, sophisticated by many considerations,

* Wealth of Nations, pp. 323–4, 328.

some absurd and some serious, some of this is bound to appear a trifle over simple.

In the first place, we do not assume automatic harmony between the disposition to save and the disposition to invest; and although opinions may differ as to the practical importance of the distinction, other things being equal, we must all agree that disharmonies are conceivable, either one way or the other; and that, if they occur, they can cause either deflation or inflation. And certainly, if deflations or inflations are taking place, then, in the former event, a downward shift in the saving function and, in the latter, an upward movement might be helpful, though the ways in which such shifts are brought about need very careful watching. Thus, although we may be sceptical about the emphasis on such movements as causes or remedies – as I personally am – the carefree assertion that saving is always beneficial needs a good deal of explicit statement regarding other assumptions before it can be accepted as satisfying the dictates of the sensitive theoretical conscience. Thus, for instance, I myself now think that exhortations to save at the bottom of the Great Depression of the 1930s were misplaced. Against this I should regard the suggestion that the severity of the depression was due to over-saving, rather than to monetary mismanagement and structural disharmonies, as equally misleading.

Secondly, as regards the behaviour of governments, it must surely be recognised that much material investment which would be regarded as sensible by most schools of thought – the types of investment mentioned at the beginning of this chapter, much of the road system, lighthouses, public buildings for various purposes, and so on, whether financed by taxes or borrowings – must almost inevitably be initiated by government whose decisions, as was indicated earlier, necessarily differ in kind from the decisions of individuals or the spontaneous decisions of groups of individuals. Even if governments are as prodigal as suggested by Adam Smith it is clear that a substantial amount of such accumulation is necessarily decided by collectivist rather than individual decision and that some at least is beneficial.

As for the influence of governments on net accumulation, the evidence of history is ambiguous, depending maybe on the form of government in vogue. In our own day we have seen, in Soviet Russia, abstinence to the point of grinding poverty, and even death by starvation, imposed on a subject people in the interest of investment in industrial development, particularly the building up of the machinery of defence and aggression. Whether this is to be regarded as impoverishment or the reverse must necessarily depend on one's scale of human values. But it is not prodigality in Adam Smith's sense. In contrast, again and again in free societies, we have seen government expenditures running ahead of the resources available in ways which, whatever their other merits, must be regarded as inimical to real investment and sometimes indeed to financial stability. Certainly it would be difficult to believe that the conduct of public finance in the United Kingdom in the years since the Second World War has been conducive to *net* accumulation.

Doubtless this last verdict may be regarded as controversial; and our qualifications of the simple majority Classical recommendations, although necessary in the interests of truth, may be thought to involve inconvenient inhibitions on clear-cut generalisations. But nothing that has been said, either with regard to possible divergencies between planned saving and planned investment or the extent of public decisions to accumulate or decumulate, should detract from the desirability of the freedom of individuals or small groups of individuals to decide the ratio between what *they* spend and what *they* save. If disharmonies occur in the capital market involving inflation or deflation, that is the business of the governments or central banks to rectify. If decisions regarding public investment exceed or fall short of what may be regarded as optimal, that is again a matter for governments or the citizens, to whom governments may or may not give heed. But I see no convincing justification for interfering with the decisions of individuals regarding the disposition of their own resources within whatever framework of general fiscal and financial policy may prevail. And I am bound to add that, when I think of the history of the last quarter of a century in my own country, I am inclined to think that many things would have been better, both as regards the volume of accumulation and the control of inflation, if there had been more scope for such decisions than the general tendency of public policy permitted or approved.

CHAPTER 3

The Organisation of Production

INTRODUCTION

As I pointed out in the first chapter, the special characteristic of the conception of the desirable shape of the economic system entertained by the Classical Economists was a comprehensive one. Given the functions of the state in maintaining law and order and providing special services which individuals or small groups were unlikely to provide, the System of Natural Liberty, as it was called by Adam Smith, involved freedom both in the realm of consumption and in the realm of production.

There was this difference, however, which, from the ideological point of view, it is important to recognise. Subject to the various qualifications mentioned already, freedom in the sphere of consumption can be regarded as an ultimate end, or at least as a prerequisite of ethical significant conduct as distinct from mechanical reaction – there will be more to say about this in the last chapter of this book. Freedom in the sphere of production may also be regarded in this light, as regards the disposition to work. But otherwise it is broadly to be considered as essentially a *means*, an organisation whose acceptability depends on its capacity to do what the consumers, including the state, wish it to do. I know no passages in which this distinction was explicitly made by the Classical writers. But I am confident that they would have admitted it; I am also confident that it is good sense.

But if this is so, if there is this dichotomy of conception, then the respective justifications must necessarily be different. It is possible to imagine a state of affairs in which there was liberty in the sphere of consumption coexisting with the absence of liberty in the sphere of production – a condition in which the means of production were collectively owned and labour was subject to direction and regulation. I hasten to say that I do not think such a state of affairs permanently viable – I shall say something about this when I discuss collectivism in general. But what I have said is perhaps enough to show that the case for liberty to choose between goods produced and to indicate by the exercise of such choice how resources should be allocated, does not settle the issue how production is to be organised.

Now, with the exception of John Stuart Mill whose ambiguities I will discuss in another chapter, the Classical answer to this question was clear. Assuming the appropriate apparatus of law and the discharge of other desirable functions of the state, they believed in private property, free enterprise and the market. At the outset of this survey I have already emphasised the central importance in their outlook of the interaction of these factors, the conception of orderly relationships, conditioned it is true by law or custom, but, within such limitations, serving the demands of individuals and groups of individuals spontaneously formulated and in no way directly dictated by central authority save in so far as it too entered the market as a buyer. It is the object of this and the following chapter to examine the grounds on which this conception rested and the criticisms to which it may be exposed.

PROPERTY AS AN ELEMENT IN PRODUCTIVE ORGANISATION – THE CLASSICAL CONCEPTION

We may begin with property since the laws relating to this institution and the contracts which can be made regarding it form part of the essential assumption of the Classical analysis of market relationships and their function.

The basic grounds for this assumption were explored at considerable length by David Hume, both in his *Treatise of Human Nature* and his *Enquiry Concerning the Principles of Morals*. Broadly speaking his position rests on two grounds. First, although it is wrong to regard men as purely self-regarding in the sense which excludes family affection and friendship of greater or lesser degrees of intimacy, a general disposition to universal benevolence is not to be relied upon. Secondly, there is a limitation on the means to meet many human wants; and, unless it is in the specific interests of individuals to look after them, there is liable to be waste and confusion. In Hume's own words in the *Treatise of Human Nature*,

> There are three different species of goods, which we are possess'd of; the internal satisfaction of our minds, the external advantages of our body, and the enjoyment of such possessions as we have acquir'd by our industry and good fortune. We are perfectly secure in the enjoyment of the first. The second may be ravish'd from us, but can be of no advantage to him who deprives us of them. The last only are both expos'd to the violence of others, and may be transferr'd without suffering any loss of alteration; while at the same time, there is not a sufficient quantity of them to supply every one's desires and necessities. As the improvement, therefore, of these goods is the chief advantage of society, so the *instability* of their possession, along with their *scarcity*, is the chief impediment [Hume's italics].

Men must therefore 'seek for a remedy, by putting these goods, as far as possible, on the same footing with the fix'd and constant advantages of the mind and body. This can be done after no other manner, than by a convention enter'd into by all the members of the society to bestow stability on the possession of those external goods, and leave everyone in the peaceable enjoyment of what he may acquire by his fortune and industry.'*

This is not necessarily an explicit promise or original contract. It is only a general sense of common interest which induces men to regulate their conduct by certain rules.

Nor is the rule concerning the stability of possession the less deriv'd from human conventions, that it arises gradually, and acquires force by a slow progression, and by our repeated experience of the inconveniences of transgressing it. On the contrary, this experience assures us still more, that the sense

* *Treatise of Human Nature,* ed. T. H. Green and T. H. Grose (London, 1882) vol. II, pp. 261–2.

of interest has become common to all our fellows, and gives us a confidence of the future regularity of their conduct: And 'tis only on the expectation of this, that our moderation and abstinence are founded. In like manner are languages gradually establish'd by human conventions without any promise. In like manner do gold and silver become the common measures of exchange, and are esteem'd sufficient payment for what is of a hundred times their value.*

Thus the rationale of property is 'utility' in the wide sense of the word. There is no question, as in much of the earlier literature, of inviolable natural rights and similar *apologia*; only a rule, liable to exceptions such as siege conditions and similar emergencies, generally conducive to the convenience of society.

Hume's positive analysis is supplemented in the works of Bentham by an extensive analysis of the evil consequences which, in his judgement, would follow the abolition of the security of property; and, until the rise of socialist criticism in the nineteenth century prompted Mill to some re-examination – of which more hereafter – it was taken more or less for granted. In this connection we may take McCulloch as reasonably representative. 'Let us not deceive ourselves,' he said, 'by supposing that it is possible for any people to emerge from barbarism, or to become wealthy, prosperous and civilised without the security of property. . . . Where it is wanting it is idle to expect either riches or civilization. . . . The right of property has not made poverty but it has powerfully contributed to make *wealth*.'†

The general position, however, received powerful support from two supplementary sources, the Theory of Population and the Theory of Capital.

So far as population was concerned, it will be remembered that the first *Essay* of Malthus on that subject, which was responsible for most of the publicity which his famous theories received, was specifically related to the prospects of society if, according to the precepts of Godwin, Condorcet and others, the institution of private property was abolished and a help-

*Ibid. p. 263. In my *Theory of Economic Policy in English Classical Political Economy*, pp. 49–55, I have given a more detailed account of Hume's position as set forth in the *Enquiries concerning the Principles of Morals*.

†*Principles of Political Economy* (1830) pp. 88–90.

yourself-as-you-please regime instituted in its stead. One of the most forceful sections of the *Essay* depicted the deterioration of conditions in a hypothetical community when, the motives for prudence having been thus removed, in two or three generations the entire population was reduced to a common subsistence level.

As is well known by the time the second edition of the *Essay* came to be written Malthus had so modified his position as to admit the possibility of a check on the multiplication which did not deserve the designation of vice or misery – the comprehensive description in the first edition of *all* influences restraining population from outrunning subsistence. And although he himself excluded deliberate birth control from this conception of what he called 'moral restraint', this view was not shared by those who supported his general thesis in other respects, Francis Place, the Mills and their successors, the neo-Malthusians. So that what had been a message of gloom concerning the future of society became, in John Stuart Mill's words, 'a banner of hope'.

But this somewhat sensational change did not involve the abandonment of the argument against the abolition of property. On the contrary, for the majority of those professing the Classical outlook, if anything it reinforced it. If 'moral restraint' was to be found anywhere, it was to be found where the institutions of private property were likely to foster it and to provide an incentive. Again John Stuart Mill was an exception, arguing that in small communist communities the pressure of public opinion against irresponsible multiplication might be expected to be greater than elsewhere. But although, with the totalitarian societies (which he would have loathed) this is conceivable, at that time this must have seemed in the region of pure hypothesis; and the example of population restraint practised by societies of property-owning peasants such as the France of that day (which he admired) must have seemed to afford considerable support for the majority view.

As regards the Theory of Capital and its relation to the institutions of property, the main Classical position was even less ambiguous. Without capital there could be little division of labour and therefore little economic growth. And although, as we have seen, it was not denied that there were desirable works of one kind or another which would not come into existence if the state did not take the initiative, it certainly was not the Classical belief that the net accumulation which made them possible was likely to be increased by positive public policy. The growth of capital in the Classical conception was essentially the result of individual action designed to increase individual holdings. The existence of the institution of private property was therefore an indispensable prerequisite of such behaviour and its absence, or limitation, would have results inimical to the increase of the income of society. According to Adam Smith in the *Wealth of Nations*,

> When we compare . . . the state of a nation at two different periods, and find, that the annual produce of its land and labour is evidently greater at the latter than at the former, that its lands are better cultivated, its manufacturers more numerous and more flourishing, and its trade more extensive, we may be assured that its capital must have increased during the interval between those two periods, and that more must have been added to it by the good conduct of some, than had been taken from it either by the private misconduct of others, or by the public extravagance of government.*

As we have seen already, there was a minority view represented by Malthus and Lauderdale, regarding the benefits of continuous accumulation, which we shall consider when discussing theories of the stability of the system as a whole. But, in the main, Adam Smith's unequivocal position was certainly shared by the majority of Classical Economists.

SELF-INTEREST AND THE MARKET

If the theory of property underlying the Classical approach owes its conspicuous formulation to David Hume, the theory of self-interest and the market is equally attributable to Adam Smith.

Who can forget the passages in the *Wealth of Nations*, so apt to be misunderstood but, properly interpreted, still so cogent, in which it is argued that the mutual dependence involved by

* Wealth of Nations, vol. I, pp. 325–6.

the division of labour is secured in general by the interests of the persons concerned.

In civilised societies man stands at all times in need of the co-operation and assistance of great multitudes, while his whole life is scarce sufficient to gain the friendship of a few persons. In almost every other race of animals each individual, when it is grown up to maturity, is entirely independent, and in its natural state has occasion for the assistance of no other living creature. But man has almost constant occasion for the help of his brethren, and it is in vain for him to expect it from their benevolence only. He will be more likely to prevail if he can interest their self-love in his favour, and show them that it is for their own advantage to do for him what he requires of them. Whoever offers to another a bargain of any kind, proposes to do this. Give me that which I want, and you shall have this which you want, is the meaning of every such offer; and it is in this manner that we obtain from one another the far greater part of those good offices which we stand in need of. It is not from the benevolence of the butcher, the brewer, or the baker, that we expect our dinner, but from their regard to their own interest. We address ourselves, not to their humanity but to their self-love, and never talk to them of our own necessities but of their advantages.*

The misunderstanding, of course, usually arises from a narrow interpretation of the concept of self-interest. It is a grotesque misconstruction to regard the author of the *Theory of Moral Sentiments* as using this term as equivalent to egotistical selfishness. Quite clearly, in this context and indeed throughout the *Wealth of Nations*, it does not mean this: it means only the interest of the individual concerned in the matters with which he is most intimately concerned. These may be of course simply his own pleasures; but equally they may involve family affections, obligations, friendships and even wider activities in which his part seems to him to be central.† It is

*Ibid. vol. I, p. 16.

†Anyone who doubts this interpretation should be referred to the direct statement of the *Theory of Moral Sentiments*, 'That account of human nature, however, which deduces all sentiments and affections from self-love, which has made so much noise in the world, but which, so far as I know has never been fully and distinctly explained, seems to me to have arisen from some confused misapprehension of the system of sympathy' – 11th edn (1805) vol. II, p. 315.

equally a travesty to present self-interest in this sense as necessarily 'materialistic'. As the power to purchase increases, it
is less rather than more likely to be attracted by 'merely
materialistic' preoccupations, whatever that means. When
Adam Smith makes self-interest in his sense the mainspring of
the economic activities of the individual, he has simply in mind
the same sort of consideration as had Alfred Marshall when
he urged that, in organising the normal work of the world,
'progress mainly depends on the extent to which the *strongest*
and not merely the *highest* forces of human nature can be
utilised for the increase of social good'.*

Given this powerful incentive, it was Smith's contention that
the operation of free markets would secure an allocation of
resources, that is to say a division of labour, tending to satisfy
what he called effectual demand. If, in any line of production,
the price prevailing is such as to secure more than the normal
rate of profit on costs of production, then there arises a tendency for producers to move in until the disparity disappears;
if the relationship is the contrary, that is prices yielding less than
normal profit or even loss, a reverse tendency is set up. Thus
'the quantity of every commodity brought to market naturally
suits itself to the effectual demand – it is the interest of all those
who employ their land, labour or stock that the quantity never
should exceed the effectual demand: and it is the interest of all
other people that it never should fall short of that demand'.† As
in such conditions the constituent elements in the cost of
production of any particular commodity would be bought at
the rates which would have to be paid for them by the producers of other products, it should be clear that we have here
an anticipation of the so-called opportunity-cost doctrine of
more recent analysis. It is a picture in which, given the initial
distribution of purchasing power due to property and the results
of past activities and transfers, economic activity is subject to
the controlling power of demand. Production is directed in
anticipation of the way in which individuals, institutions and
governments are expected to spend their money.

Thus viewed in its broadest perspective the 'System of

*Marshall, *Industry and Trade*, 4th edn (London: Macmillan, 1923) p. 664. The
italics are D. H. Robertson's who inserts them in his citation of Marshall in his
Utility and All That (London: Allen & Unwin, 1952) p. 45.

†*Wealth of Nations*, vol. 1, p. 59.

Natural Liberty', from the point of view of productive organisation, presents a conception of decentralised initiative in sharp contrast to systems directed from the centre. Central organisation was indeed assumed in the shape of law within which initiative was possible; and it was also assumed that there were positive functions where central control was incumbent. But over the larger part of the field it was the institutions of property and markets and the spontaneous interests of individuals or groups of individuals which gave rise to an organisation of production which in the last analysis was controlled by effective demand.

It should be clearly realised that this conception presupposed (in its ideal state) liberty, 'the freedom of the trader' to change his trade as often as he pleases' – to quote Adam Smith. No one could have denounced what he called 'The Policy of Europe',* the policy which allowed statutory corporations and markets restricted by tariff or other kinds of regulations to distort the operation of the price system, with greater astringency than he did. But it should also be noted that he did not think that the prevalence of such policies rendered nugatory the existence of markets and their effect on the decision of labour. As he explains, commenting on the outlook of his French contemporaries, the Physiocrats,

> Some speculative physicians seem to have imagined that the health of the human body could be preserved only by a certain precise regimen of diet and exercise, of which every, the smallest, violation necessarily occasioned some degree of disease or disorder proportioned to the degree of violation. Experience, however, would seem to show that the human body frequently preserves, to all appearances at least, the most perfect state of health under a vast variety of different regimens; even under some which are generally believed to be very far from being perfectly wholesome. But the healthful state of the human body, it would seem, contains in itself some unknown principle of preservation, capable either of preventing or of correcting, in many respects, even the bad effects of a very faulty regimen. Mr Quesnai, who was himself a physician, and a very speculative physician, seems

*Ibid. vol. I, p. 58.

to have entertained a notion of the same kind concerning the political body, and to have imagined that it would thrive and prosper only under a certain precise regimen, the exact regimen of perfect liberty and perfect justice. He seems not to have considered that in the political body the natural effort which every man is continually making to better his own condition is a principle of preservation capable of preventing and correcting, in many respects, the bad effects of a political economy, in some degree both partial and oppressive. Such a political economy, though it no doubt retards more or less, is not always capable of stopping altogether the natural progress of a nation towards wealth and prosperity, and still less of making it go backwards. If a nation could not prosper without the enjoyment of perfect liberty and perfect justice, there is not in the world a nation which could ever have prospered. In the political body, however, the wisdom of nature has fortunately made ample provision for remedying many of the bad effects of the folly and injustice of man; in the same manner as it has done in the natural body, for remedying those of his sloth and intemperance.*

It follows therefore that the praise of the invisible hand of the market by which the individual 'is led to promote an end which was no part of his intention', so often made the pretext for ridicule by the ignorant, was in no sense to be regarded as approbation of contemporary reality, limited and constricted as Smith thought it to be by contemporary law favouring monopolistic restrictions. It was rather the recognition of forces which, if not so limited and constricted, would have, in his opinion, the effect of evoking an organisation of production in harmony with the forces of demand. The invisible hand worked in a beneficial direction; but its operations were often frustrated by adverse influences.

Suppose, however, that these adverse influences were not present. Suppose the 'Policy of Europe' to be supplanted by the 'System of Natural Liberty' working with the framework of law and institutions recommended in the *Wealth of Nations*. Would we say, from the standpoint of further speculation and

*Ibid. vol. II, p. 172.

experience, that no supplementations or limitations were desirable from the point of view of productive organisation? That is the question to which the remainder of the chapter and the whole of the next will be devoted.

EXTERNAL DISECONOMIES

We may begin our survey by ignoring those more recent developments of the forms of property and the market where we shall probably find most criticism or extension of the Classical position to be necessary, and, assuming the institutional pattern of Adam Smith's day, ask whether what has already been said is in need of further glosses or reservations before the claims made for that position can be said to be justified.

The answer to this question must certainly be no. Even taking account of the stated requirements of an appropriate legal framework as well as the activities of the state, the claims made for the organisation of production through market forces do not explicitly recognise the possibility of adverse side-effects of particular operations which must be taken into account on any aggregate assessment. I refer, of course, to use technical jargon, to the so-called external diseconomies of production – the pollution of rivers by poisonous effluents, the damage done by the emission of dirt into the air, and so on.

There is no need to spend much time on the problems raised by such phenomena. There is no doubt of the possibility of their existence and that on a very damaging scale; and their nature is closely akin to the external diseconomies of consumption already discussed at some little length above. There is equally no doubt that the Classical Economists would have admitted the desirability of their control. Adam Smith makes allusion to the justification of regulations regarding the danger of the spreading of fires.* Pigou's illustration of the difference between private and social net product in terms of smoke nuisance has been the common currency of the so-called Welfare Economics for more than half a century. The perpetual emergence of writers and speakers who talk about such questions as though they were a recent discovery – sometimes indeed *their own*

*Ibid. vol. I, p. 307.

discovery – may be a salutary reminder of the time it takes for any important problem to be generally recognised; but it is also evidence of the extraordinary provincialism in time of much contemporary professional literature. The detailed problems of control, the weighing of costs against benefits and the administration necessary to curb particular diseconomies differ greatly in each manifestation, and are likely to be at a maximum where the evil spreads over different national borders. But, on the plane of generality of this essay, it can confidently be said that no one but a fool, or a person with sinister interest, would deny the desirability in principle of control of free enterprise in this connection. The prevention of nuisances of this order should be regarded as part of the necessary framework of law and order.

It is, however, perhaps desirable to point out, what is not so frequently recognised, that in part at least of this problem – and I repeat the qualification 'in part' – this is just another aspect of a much more tremendous problem, the problem of population. There are doubtless problems of particular diseconomies both of consumption and production which arise even where the ratio of population to the relevant land and sea resources is small. But many become the serious problems which they are today only when the ratio is much greater. The fish can stand mild doses of effluents without great danger of depletion of numbers; but they cannot stand all that much. Some degree of noise may even cheer some people up; but beyond a certain point it begins to be intolerable. Considered from this point of view it should be clear that the control of external diseconomies presents many (and complex) problems. But the proposition that, if it is to serve social ends which are desirable, the invisible hand has to move within limits which preclude gross diseconomies of the kind discussed here, does not present great intellectual difficulties.*

---

*This is not to argue that there are not very considerable difficulties in devising and administering policies which are directed to this end. On such matters see William J. Baumol and Wallace Oates, *The Theory of Environmental Policy* (New York: Harcourt & Brace, 1975).

EXTERNAL ECONOMIES: INFANTS AND INVALIDS

Much greater difficulties arise in the sphere of positive side-effects – the so-called 'external' economies of production. The general position in this connection is that the development of certain activities may carry with it beneficial effects not entering into the calculations of immediate profitability of those responsible and, further, that in such cases there are grounds for public support in the shape of subsidies or tariff protection to promote their existence.

The standard analysis here was argued by Hamilton and List in pleas for the protection of infant industry in the countries with which they were concerned and it was developed with incomparably greater subtlety and philosophical range, as a direct critique of Adam Smith, by that unfortunate neglected genius, John Rae.* As is well known, probably under the influence of Rae, it was admitted as an exception to the case against protection by John Stuart Mill – though his support of tariffs rather than subsidies was later withdrawn because of the uses to which his arguments had been put by sinister interest.† The context of this discussion related specifically to tariffs and subsidies in international trade. But it could be generalised for communities within which there prevail marked inter-local differences of mobility and education, though the political and administrative difficulties would probably be greater.

The trouble about such contentions is at once practical and intellectual. The practical argument is simple; once concede the support, whether by tariff or subsidy, to the activities in question and it tends to stick. The infants become giants and the support continues – an obvious misdirection of resources. More than a century and a half after Hamilton's splendid *Report on Manufactures* the United States continues to be a protectionist country.

The intellectual problem is more complex, namely how to

*His *New Principles of Political Economy* (1834), fortunately made available by the Toronto University Press (1965), is in my judgement by far the most profound critique of the Smithian system in any language known to me.

†*Principles of Political Economy*, ed. J. Robson (Toronto University Press, 1965) pp. 918–19.

measure such side-effects and balance them against the costs involved. There is clearly no simple mode of quantification: attempts to do so should be usually regarded as bogus. It is certainly not difficult to conceive of areas where the impulse to entrepreneurial independence is so little present that some paternalistic initiative of this sort may be justified – though actual experience with the so-called under-developed countries suggests that, in many cases, the initiative tends to be grotesquely misdirected, often, alas, on the advice of Western economists. As for more-developed areas, I find it difficult to believe that there are many instances where such artificial fostering of industry can be commended on grounds of general interest: in such communities the educational function is probably better discharged in other ways. Exceptions are conceivable, notably in the sphere of defence industries. But experience suggests that the actual cases which occur are much more likely to be the result of sectional pressures than considerations of the common good.

It is conceivable that the concept of external economies might be invoked, not merely in favour of the support of *infant*, but also of *invalid* industries. It is easy to imagine the ingredients of the analysis, the loss of industrial skills, the discouragement of research in particular lines, the additional burden in local taxation, and so on and so forth. Do we not hear arguments of this sort whenever any industrial group gets into difficulties nowadays? – the only thing occasionally missing is the appeal to more pretentious conceptions and jargon. In my judgement, however, the argument is even less convincing in regard to invalids than it is in regard to infants. It may be conceded that, in the present disorganised state of international relations, it may be necessary to sustain at a loss certain industrial concerns catering for the indiscriminate benefit of defence; and, unfortunately, with the growing complexity of defence techniques, this group of exceptions is much larger than it was in the days when Adam Smith defended the Navigation Acts on the ground that defence was more than opulence. But outside this area the case is very weak. Admittedly, when an industrial group becomes unprofitable, there are all sorts of adverse side-effects of the kind already mentioned. But if the difficulties are genuinely temporary, it will be very surprising if help is not forthcoming from normal financial quarters – in which case the side-effects will not occur. And if they are not, then unless it is desired to preserve for ever what has proved to be an inappropriate allocation of resources, it is far better to meet the adverse side-effects in other ways – assistance to mobility, temporary relief of the rate burden and the like. It must be the most exceptional disaster or the most inexplicable failure of all concerned to discern the temporary nature of the invalidity which can justify the relief being given *via* the invalid industry. Generalisation of such assistance must lead in the end to losses which make more difficult the provision of relief in more suitable ways. At present we have not to go far from home to see the very real danger of policies which impede the adaptation of industry to changing conditions of demand and supply.

PROPERTY AND MANAGEMENT

We now come to problems which, although doubtless they existed in the Classical period, seem to have become much more conspicuous since then and at least to demand some reconsideration of the Classical outlook. The next chapter will be wholly devoted to such problems in so far as they relate to market structure and monopolistic association. But problems which arise from changing relationships between ownership and initiative are more conveniently dealt with in the immediate context of the Classical theories of property and self-interest.

In his exposition of the utility of property, David Hume showed himself to be not at all unaware of the variety of laws and customs in this respect: it was indeed this circumstance which led him to ridicule the idea of any simple archetypal, natural right in this connection. But he placed no emphasis on what was to be the most conspicuous development of the future: the rise of property in joint-stock companies. Nor is there any recognition of the potentialities of this form of organisation in the *Wealth of Nations*. As we shall see, Adam Smith had a very poor view of what they could do outside a very restricted field. It is no accident that neither the discussions of the division of labour in book I nor of the accumulation of capital in book II contain any extended reference to this form of property holding. The discussion, such as it is, of joint-stock companies and their scope comes in book v which deals with the functions of the state.

Now, of course, at the time of Adam Smith, and for nearly three-quarters of a century afterwards, the growth of this form of organisation, although quite considerable, was restrained by the absence of limited liability. While the investor who placed any resources in such a company was held responsible by law to the extent of all his property for all its debts, this was an obvious disincentive to the rate of growth. Yet some at least of the Classical Economists were opposed to its removal. Powerful figures such as Overstone and McCulloch held the principle of limitation to be immoral. John Stuart Mill's view that, provided the invitation was explicit, there was no moral objection was by no means universally accepted. It took almost endless pamphleteering and public enquiry for this obvious truism to get through.*

But Adam Smith's reserves did not lie in this universe of discourse. His strong distaste for state-supported monopolies, especially those long established in foreign trade, led him, albeit illogically, to develop strong general objections to the joint-stock principle in general save in exceptional cases. He argued that,

> To buy in one market and to sell, with profit, in another, when there are many competitors in both; to watch over, not only the occasional variations in the demand, but the much greater and more frequent variations in the competition, or in the supply which that demand is likely to get from other people, and to suit with dexterity and judgement both the quantity and quality of each assortment of goods to all these circumstances, is a species of warfare of which the operations are continually changing, and which can scarce ever be conducted successfully, without such an unremitting exertion of vigilance and attention, as cannot long be expected from the directors of a joint stock company.†

The exceptional cases were banking, fire and income insurance, canals and water supply; and the reason for their

*For a fuller account of this controversy see my *Theory of Economic Development in the History of Economic Thought* (London: Macmillan, 1968) pp. 105–8.

†*Wealth of Nations*, vol. I, p. 245.

exception, according to Smith, was that their operations were 'capable of being reduced to what is called a routine, or to such a uniformity of method as admits of little or no variation'.

Judged in the light of subsequent developments this sounds more than a little ridiculous. Indeed as Scott argued with some cogency in his famous *Joint Stock Companies to 1720*,* it is very doubtful whether it was plausible as an evaluation of history prior to the eighteenth century. But to contend that, outside the limited field indicated by Smith, this form of organisation has shown itself to be uniformly, or mainly, incapable of efficiency or initiative does not carry conviction. The sort of person who writes popular books, or gives popular broadcasts, guying the economic thought of the past would find it easy to have an absolute field-day at Smith's expense in this respect.

Nevertheless it is clear that with the emergence of this type of organisation, possibilities of disharmonies between the interests of management and the shareholders do certainly exist; and, although Smith's dogmatic assertions regarding the capacities of boards of directors are highly vulnerable both historically and as general propositions, there can be no doubt that where the interests of the original investors are not under their own individual supervision, important and complex questions arise concerning the nature and the incentives of their representation.

Now in my opinion, it would be very wrong to argue that substantial financial interests, other than fees and salaries, are a *sine qua non* of efficiency and regard to the interests of shareholders in the conduct of public companies. Certainly many examples could be quoted to the contrary: and, given the complexities of human motivation, it is not to be excluded that, over a not negligible part of the field, incentives other than participation in the residue, positive or negative, of receipts over expenditure – public spirit, conscientious obligation, civic honours and so on – may be reasonably effective. It is, however, probably true that historically, at least, many of the most successful corporations owe their initiation and success to the efforts of directors who have had a large share in the equity; and the fact that, at the present time, there is a widespread call for retention of the possibility of share options for management

*W. R. Scott, *Joint Stock Companies to 1720*, vol. 1, pp. 448–58.

is evidence for the view that, even at this level, the existence of a cash incentive has some value. It may operate *less intermittently* than the prospect of a place in the honours list or even conscientious obligation; and it deserves to be said explicitly that the desire to do well for one's wife and family is not so contemptible a motive as some modern moralists would have us believe.

Furthermore, although there are conspicuous instances of the success of undertakings where management has been more or less hereditary or recruitment has been limited to restricted circles, there have been many examples where the contrary outcome was to be observed. The prevalence of the guinea-pig director is apt to be exaggerated nowadays. Public opinion is usually at least a quarter of a century behind reality in these matters; and the extent to which the boards of leading companies are populated by technicians, lawyers, accountants and men who have got where they are the hard way up, is not yet sufficiently realised. The so-called media positively revel in fiction resting on this kind of misconception. But clearly the possibility of intellectually and morally inadequate representation of the shareholder interest has existed and still exists.

In any case, it is not difficult in general to conceive instances where the interests of boards and their shareholders may diverge. The desire for a quiet life rather than quick adaptation to change, a failure to perceive opportunities for profit visible to other competent persons, a disposition arbitrarily to reinvest funds which might well be paid out to the shareholders – these and dozens of other possibilities are the common currency of knowledgeable discussion of such matters.

Doubtless the answer to some of this is that it is always open to shareholders to choose other management. But shareholders are not always sufficiently alive to their own interests. In forming judgement on the complicated operations of modern corporations, the individual or minority group is often at a disadvantage compared with the executive. This is a sort of situation in which it can be argued that the possibility of takeover bids by groups which specialise in scrutinising the field for such opportunities is a useful check on the existing management. It concentrates the mind wonderfully to know that Mr X or Lord Y has his eye on your balance sheet. But the takeover business itself is liable to abuses – although it is often itself unjustly abused – and it would be too easy a view of the scene of corporate enterprise in the modern world to argue that the law or informal regulation has yet made them unlikely to occur.

Taking a broad view of what has happened in this respect in the field of joint enterprise over the years since the introduction of limited liability, I would venture the generalisation that much, although doubtless not sufficient, has been done to eliminate the disharmonies of interest of the kind under discussion, especially as regards the responsibility for choice regarding the reinvestment of profits. But – and this is a moral not frequently drawn explicitly – this has certainly been due to modifications and extensions of law and informally admini- stered sanctions, rather than by direct intervention by govern- ments and their representatives in the conduct of particular undertakings. The ramifications of company law, as has been found to be necessary in different parts of the world, can indeed be quoted against those naïve spirits who hold that the neces- sary legal prescriptions for a truly free-enterprise system can be inscribed briefly on a few tablets of stone. But equally they can be adduced to show that it is by the elaboration of general rules within which free decisions can be made rather than by detailed prescription of decisions from central authority that orderly progress can be made in this connection. There is still much wisdom in Adam Smith's opinion that

> The statesman, who should attempt to direct private people in what manner they ought to employ their capitals, would not only load himself with a most unnecessary attention, but assume an authority which could safely be trusted, not only to no single person, but to no council or senate whatever, and which would nowhere be so dangerous as in the hands of a man who had folly and presumption enough to fancy himself fit to exercise it.*

Wealth of Nations, vol. i, p. 421.

CHAPTER 4

The Organisation of Production (continued)

COMPETITION AND MONOPOLY

We may now turn to questions relating to wider aspects of the organisation of production in market economies – to questions relating to the degree to which there may arise in this area the desirability of central regulation over and above the provision of an evolving framework of law and order.

Let me begin by disposing of a misapprehension. It is sometimes argued nowadays that the case for the market economy rests essentially upon the assumption of perfect competition in the sense in which that state of affairs is conceived in mathematical models. This is not so. I am quite sure that if it had been so said to a representative Classical Economist, still more, let us say, to Alfred Marshall who certainly understood the mathematics of the subject, it would have been rejected; and in my opinion rightly so too. I say nothing against the mathematical models in question: they have served a useful purpose in enabling us to put precision into the analysis of certain hypothetical abstract relationships. But the conception which underlay the Classical commendation of the working of the competitive market economy was something at once less exacting and more comprehensive than this.

It was less exacting in that it certainly did not rely on the assumption that all supplies were in the hands of units whose proportionate contributions to total output were so small that isolated individual variations had no effect on prices so that, for them, therefore, marginal revenue and price were the same. That simplification may have helped for certain purposes

of exposition, as explicitly explained by Marshall in the famous 'Note XIV' in the 'Mathematical Appendix' in his *Principles.**
But it carried no presumption that things were always, or ever, predominantly so in real life.

Moreover, in so far as it carried an implication that in order that competition should exist it was necessary for the number of productive units to be large, it was apt to be very misleading. In many branches of productive activity, probably in most, the single-product firm, so beloved of elementary textbook exposition, is the exception rather than the rule. This is so, even in agriculture; and to imagine the contrary is to be liable to an immense under-estimate of elasticities of supply. The practically important quality of a competitive situation is not that there shall be a large number of *actual* suppliers, but rather that, if any actual supplier is doing particularly well, there is a reasonable possibility of other *potential* suppliers coming in and competing away the abnormal profits. And this is much more likely in a world of many-product firms, where starting up supplies may involve quite minor switches of organisation, than in a regime of more specialised units where an increase of supply may involve large capital outlays before this can begin.

But beyond this – and it is here that greater comprehensiveness comes in – if we conceive the market economy not merely as an apparatus for supplying more or less static and known demands but rather as an agent for dynamic growth – which certainly was the Classical conception – it is surely clear that, at any moment, it *must* include elements which are not part of the conception of competition in any narrow sense of the term. Every time that an innovation is introduced, there emerges, *pro tem*, a monopolistic position; indeed it is the prospects of achieving the advantages of such a position which, in part at least, is one of the spurs to innovation, either of processes or products. Certainly no sensible idea of a desirable market economy would wish this possibility out of the picture. The important thing, from this point of view, is not that monopoly

---

*Alfred Marshall, *Principles of Economics*, 9th edn (London: Macmillan, 1961) p. 849. See my *Evolution of Modern Economic Theory* (London: Macmillan, 1970) pp. 30–1 for some account of the almost unbelievable misapprehensions concerning the origin of the distinction between marginal revenue and price.

in this sense should not *emerge*, but rather that it should not *persist*.*

MONOPOLY AND MONOPOLISTIC PRACTICES – THE NATURE OF THE PROBLEM

But the monopoly problem arises in forms much more substantial than those of the transitory results of innovation and goodwill: and although in some cases it is possible to exaggerate the ill effects, usually where it persists it must be regarded as a distorting factor in the allocation of resources. The fundamental diagnosis of this influence has never been more succinctly stated than by Adam Smith in the self-same chapter as that in which he exhibits the functions of the price system in competitive markets. 'The monopolists', he says, 'by keeping the market constantly under-stocked, by never fully satisfying the effectual demand, sell their commodities much above the natural price, and raise their emoluments, whether they consist in wages or profit, greatly above their natural rate.'†

Now it cannot be said that these evils were ignored by the Classical Economists. The pages of the *Wealth of Nations* are strewn with disparaging remarks about the effects of monopolies. 'Monopoly . . . is a great enemy to good management which can never be universally established but in consequence of that free and universal competition which forces everybody to have recourse to it for the sake of self defence.'‡ They 'derange more or less the natural distribution of the stock of the country'.§ They are unjust. 'The cruellest of our revenue laws . . . are mild and gentle, in comparison of some of those which the clamour of our merchants and manufacturers has extorted from the legislature, for the support of their own absurd and

---

*The emphasis on emergent monopoly as development runs parallel to some extent with Joseph Schumpeter's analysis in chapter VIII in his famous *Capitalism, Socialism and Democracy* (New York: Harper & Row, 1969); but, as will be seen from the last sentence and what follows in the next sections, I am far from following his contention that monopolistic practices serve a necessary and positive function in the working of an acceptable market economy.

† *Wealth of Nations*, vol. I, p. 63.

‡ Ibid. vol. II, p. 148.

§ Ibid. vol. II, p. 130.

oppressive monopolies. Like the laws of Draco, these laws may be said to be all written in blood.'*

This attitude was widespread among his successors. In the well-known chapter on 'Value and Riches' in his *Principles* Ricardo expatiated further upon the distributional effect of monopoly – if there were a monopoly of water, then the rest of the community would be impoverished to the extent that the monopolist was enriched.† And again in the *Notes on Malthus* he enquires, 'If the larger gains . . . of the individual manufacturer be desirable, then is it [*sic*] an argument for a general system of monopolies – a system which considers only the profits of capitalists, and is little solicitous about the comforts and advantages of consumers.'‡ McCulloch, expatiating on the rights of property, argues that 'All monopolies which give to a few individuals the power of carrying on certain branches of industry to the exclusion of others, are thus, in fact, established in direct violation of the property of everyone else. They prevent them from using their natural capacities or powers in what they might have considered the best manner; and as every man not a slave is justly held to be the best, and indeed the only, judge of what is advantageous for himself, the most obvious principles of justice and the right of property are both subverted when he is excluded from employment.'§ And finally J. S. Mill, in his *Principles*, declares that 'to confer monopoly upon a producer or dealer, or upon a set of producers or dealers not too numerous to combine, is to give them the power of levying any amount of taxation on the public for their individual benefit which will not make the public forgo the use of the commodity'.¶

All this is pretty strong stuff; and it may be contended that it still has great relevance to the conduct of policy in our own day, with its statutory marketing agencies, its exclusive professional organisations, and some features at any rate of the operations of trade unions. Where restrictions on entry or price competition are operated by organised producers or by governments influenced by organised producers, there the presumption holds that other would-be producers are compelled to operate at

*Ibid. vol. ii, p. 146.
† *Works*, ed. Sraffa, vol. i, p. 227.
‡ Ibid. vol. ii, p. 409.
§ *Principles of Political Economy*, new edn (1843) p. 81.
¶ *Principles of Political Economy* (Toronto University Press, 1965).

margins inferior, in some sense or other, to those at which they would have expected to operate had competition been free. Therefore, unless their expectations were mistaken they are condemned to lower standards of living. Nevertheless such pronouncements do not cover the whole field. They may have been the most practically relevant in the days of Adam Smith and his immediate successors; and it is arguable, even in the present day, that quantitatively more wealth has been spilt by such state-created monopolies than by any spontaneous restriction in the sphere of private enterprise. But in modern times there are other manifestations of monopoly which have the same ultimate effect but which spring from causes other than the direct action or the fostering activities of the state.

What are these manifestations? It is tempting at first to point to size as such since the size of industrial units has increased so much since the Classical period. But this is a false scent. Size as such is of little significance until it is considered in relation to the market. A giant enterprise may be subject to keen competition; a smaller one may not. And even if the giant is not subject to actual competition, it may still act as if it were, if only for reasons of prudence. What is fundamental from the point of view of the general welfare is *not size but restriction* – a volume of output less than would be probable if the field were open to production by persons or groups of persons other than the monopolist. Size in relation to markets may indeed be among the factors involving restriction. But to establish perspective in this connection it is necessary to analyse such influences more precisely.

PATENTS

We may first consider the existence of patent rights. This was certainly not unknown in the Classical period; indeed, it involved much controversy both before and at that time. But it is probably true to say that, recently, it has become both more widespread and more important as an influence conducive to power in markets and thus affecting the structure of industry. To have a set of patents intimately related to the production of a group of products is certainly a possible basis for a position of considerable monopoly power.

Now it is clear that property in knowledge, which is essentially what patent rights are, is an institution whose justification must rest on grounds other than property in material goods.* For although knowledge is scarce, in the sense that we do not know nearly enough about nearly everything, *existing* knowledge is not scarce, in the sense that its utilisation by one person does not diminish its availability for utilisation by others, if they are allowed to do so. Any scarcity in this field, therefore, which arises from patent rights is not due to material limitations; it is something which is imposed by law. Much existing knowledge in many fields is subject to no such limitations; and much new knowledge is similarly freely available as it emerges. A man engaged on fundamental research publishes his results if he is successful; he achieves some reputation in his profession and he may, or may not, receive some modest recompense. But thereafter, although there may occur bad blood and mutual recrimination about priorities – a well-known academic disease – there is no question of any restraint on the use of the discovery.

But this is no argument against the grant of patents in certain limited technological fields. It is perhaps an open question to what extent in the past the individual inventor has been mainly interested in pecuniary gain, though it is difficult to believe that this has not happened fairly frequently. But it is clear that a good deal of the systematic research involving large outlays undertaken by industrial firms would not be undertaken if there were no such incentive; and although in the nature of things it is very difficult to weigh the advantages to society of prospective discovery against what might be done with the resources so employed if they were free for other things, it seems reasonable to suppose that in many cases society is the gainer. If this is so, there is therefore a sound utilitarian argument for the grant of some temporary exclusive privilege, even though this may serve to buttress some degree of monopoly.

However, what form this should take involves technical and legal problems of no mean complexity. For how long should a patent be granted? What degree of differentiation should justify

*See the important article by Sir Arnold Plant, 'The Economic Theory concerning Patents for Inventions', *Economica*, n.s. no. 1 (Feb 1934) pp. 30–51, reprinted in his *Selected Essays and Addresses* (London: Routledge, 1974).

its renewal? At what stage should would-be competitors be allowed to utilise the knowledge in question, subject to licence payments? To what extent should the accumulation of patent rights be allowed to proceed if the domination of important markets is involved? These are still questions of acute controversy: and it is clear that no short answer applicable to all cases is available. This must be a source of disquiet to all who crave for simple solutions to all problems; and on general grounds it would certainly be desirable that further clarification of thought and practice should be achieved. But the lack of consensus in matters of detail should not affect the main conclusion that here is an important sphere of activity where some kind of temporary monopoly is probably in the public interest.

TECHNOLOGICAL FACTORS

Beyond this, however, there are spheres of activity where the brute facts of technology involve monopolistic positions which may endanger the interests of consumers. Where technique necessarily involves very large units if production is to be economically efficient or even possible, then there clearly exists the possibility that the size of the optimal productive installation may be so great that the existing market comes under monopolistic domination. The idea, prevalent in many quarters, that this state of affairs is more or less universal in the modern world, that the progress of technology inevitably leads to monopoly is, of course, ill-conceived – the degree of competition which exists, still more the degree which would exist if monopoly were not state-supported, is much greater than is commonly supposed by those who get their perspective from political novelists or popular broadcasters and television personalities. Nevetheless there are problems here whose extent was certainly not fully appreciated by the Classical writers.

In many instances the problems are artificial. A domestic market may be dominated by monopoly simply because access to it is limited by import duties or other such protective devices. If competing imports were allowed, monopolistic domination would be non-existent. In such cases the obvious remedy is to remove the protection. The extent to which part at least of the monopoly problem has been created by the fiscal policies of international trade is not to be under-estimated.

Recognition of this obvious fact, however, must not blind us to important areas where the existence of monopolistic situations arising from the technical conditions of production are not due to such influences. Where the supply of certain services, gas, electricity, rail transport, dock and airport facilities, and so on, involve the use of stretches or patches of the earth's surface or air over that surface, which often can only be acquired by compulsory purchase, then both legal and technical considerations combine to make monopolistic conditions of supply, if not absolutely inevitable, in practice an overwhelming probability. Here, because of such conditions, there is no guarantee whatsoever that, in the absence of some form of social control, the interests of the owners will necessarily harmonise with the interests of society.

It is here, I think, that one becomes conscious of a real deficiency in the Classical perspective. It is true that Adam Smith discussed roads and canals and that John Stuart Mill wrote an important tract on the London water supply and gave some cursory attention to railways. But considering the proportion of investment which, at least by the middle of the nineteenth century, was going into undertakings of this sort, and the special problems of control which almost inevitably arise in that connection, it is, I think, a legitimate reproach, at any rate to the second generation of Classical writers, that they devoted so little attention to such matters and that in their recommendations of a free-enterprise system – which still have much persuasive force – they did not indicate the extent to which, in the nature of things, public authority was involved in the provision of services quantitatively so important to the general welfare. In this way the door was left open to the Fabian outlook which tended – and still tends – to regard all problems of industrial organisation as on all fours with the public utility problem – an error of perspective certainly more fateful than any omissions in the Classical outlook.

That, however, is past history. For us, at present, the problem still remains how to deal with such situations. Two main types of policy are conceivable: either outright public ownership, or the grant of limited franchise on strict conditions to joint-stock companies. There are plenty of examples of each in contemporary economies. In some circles deserving of respect the former solution, nationalisation or municipalisation, municipal ownership is preferred – very often, I fancy, on grounds of ideology rather than productive efficiency. I personally incline towards the latter. But these are questions which can more conveniently be dealt with at a later stage when dealing with Collectivism in general.

CARTELS AND COMBINATIONS

The types of monopolistic situation discussed in the two preceding sections certainly give rise to problems of control; if they are not subject to special rules and limitations, then obviously there may be damage to the general interest. But at least it can be said that they arise from circumstances which may be said to favour production. Thus the monopolies created by patent rights can be defended on the ground that they provide incentives for the discovery of processes and products which otherwise would not be forthcoming. Again, monopolistic positions created by the technical requirements of certain kinds of productive activities do make available services not otherwise produced save at greater cost. If it were not for the incentive provided by patents, some at least of the most remarkable mechanical inventions of modern times might not have been made. If there had been no compulsory purchase powers for the acquisition of the necessary strips of land, powers almost inevitably involving the creation of monopoly, some transport services and some supplies of various kinds of power would not have come into being.

No such creative aspect can be assigned to associations of producers whose purpose it is to maintain prices above the normal competitive level, either by regulating what they charge themselves or by excluding the competition of others. In either case the net effect is to keep production at a level lower than otherwise would be the case and, by maintaining profits above what would prevail under competition, to level what Adam Smith called 'an absurd tax' on the rest of the community and, at the same time, compelling other producers to work at inferior margins.

The same verdict must be passed upon closer business combinations whose aim is to control a sufficient proportion of supplies to procure effective domination of the outlets for their products and to be in a position, by manipulating prices and other such manoeuvres, to exclude effective competition. It is important not to exaggerate the frequency of such positions. Abnormal profits have a tendency to elicit competition from unexpected quarters; and by no means all business amalgamations have domination of the market as their main intention. The pleas of sharing overheads, greater provision for research, consolidation of sources of finance for new developments, though often abused, are not all to be dismissed as mere window-dressing. But the aim to enlarge the control of markets is a persistent factor in many kinds of business; and, where it succeeds, it is at least liable to the abuses under discussion.

Now, as we have seen, such abuses were not ignored by the Classical Economists for whom the term 'monopoly' had a wholly pejorative significance. But in those days, outside the public-utility field to which, as I have said already, they gave insufficient attention, the structure of industry was such that, in the absence of support in some form or other from the government, cartel-like associations of producers were likely to be unstable and ephemeral, and combinations sufficiently large to dominate unprotected markets were infrequent. The weight of the Classical prescriptions in this connection, therefore, was directed against the public support of monopoly, either by the direct grant of exclusive privilege or the indirect support afforded by high protection. In my judgement it is probable that, confronted with later developments in industrial and commercial structure, they would have favoured positive restraints upon monopoly and monopolistic practices other than those arising from artificial support. But such measures were not in their main perspective.

In recent times, however, the position has altered. As I have argued already, it is still probably the case that, on a broad view, the greater part of monopolistic restriction owes its origin, directly or indirectly, to the policies of governments under the influence of the arts and stratagems of pressure groups – one has only to think of the nearly universal molly-coddling of agriculture in industrial countries to realise the quantitative significance of all this. But it still remains true that it is no longer sensible to assume that all cartels and combinations are liable to disintegrate or to argue that, in some cases at least, the restrictive influence of unsupported monopoly is too small to bother about or to need direct intervention by government.

But what form should such intervention take? The idea of a simple law prohibiting monopolistic behaviour in all its manifestations and capable of administration by the ordinary courts is attractive to ardent spirits. But it is ill-adapted to the complexities of real life. 'Restraint of trade' and the 'public interest' are abstract notions which need to be tested against many instances before their implications are sufficiently explicit to be made the basis of suitable action. Not all actions apparently in restraint of trade necessarily have such long-term effects – though many undoubtedly do. Not all producers' associations or combinations are necessarily against the public interest – though many unquestionably are. To spell out in advance all the possible categories of blameworthy or defensible action is a task which hitherto has defied the best efforts of legislative draughtsmen. To define beforehand the not infrequently unique circumstances of potential monopolistic situations and to judge their status from the point of view of the public interest is a problem not yet solved.

In the United Kingdom the evolution of policy in this respect has been twofold. There is a Restrictive Practices Court administering a general law covering this area and a Monopolies Commission which examines and makes recommendations upon existing organisations and proposed mergers. This division of labour has the recommendation that, through the Court, there can be built up a body of case law providing precise guidance to future practice while, through the Commission, the unique features of particular proposals of organisation can be dealt with according to what is judged to be their merits or demerits. How this compares with arrangements elsewhere, such as in the United States, where the legal complications are truly formidable, it is as yet too early to say. But the conception seems to be on lines which are conformable at once with the requirements of the general theory of policy and with the dictates of good sense. In matters of this sort it is desirable to keep in mind both the maxim *de minimis non curat lex* and also the general presumption that the *apologia* of interested parties in such contexts are to be viewed with considerable suspicion. We should not be too fussy when some probably transitory monopoly emerges. Nor should we be taken in by the claims of greater stability of markets, more efficient deployment of labour and capital, and so on – the too-often self-styled expert pleas of those who have financial interest in restriction.

TRADE UNIONS

There is one set of manifestations of monopolistic influence in the modern world which deserves some special mention. I refer to combinations of workers and employers and the practice of collective bargaining.

There is no need to spend much time on combinations on the employers' side of the labour market. Times have changed since, in the *Wealth of Nations*, Adam Smith could accuse the employers of being in a continuous tacit combination to depress wages to the lowest level consistent with common humanity. Nowadays when employers are not bidding against one another to attract the scarcer kinds of labour, their combinations, more often than not, are fairly unstable defensive associations which may, or may not, speak with one voice. The unions, however, have gathered strength and, for good or for bad, represent quite special problems in the modern world.

In this connection the position both of Classical and Neoclassical Liberalism is ambiguous. In Britain the Classical Economists defended the liberty of association. They did not think that the unions had great power to raise the level of wages above that which would be established in free markets, although the allegation that they believed in complete rigidity of the 'wage fund' is greatly exaggerated; and they gave support to the repeal of the Combination Acts, the savage law which made associations of workers a criminal offence. In his *Principles of Political Economy*, John Stuart Mill even developed a somewhat sophisticated *apologia* for the closed shop, on the grounds that it saved certain groups from the consequences of uncontrolled population growth. But in the early 1830s Senior developed strong objections to violence in picketing and restrictive practices; and, apart from the special argument already mentioned, Mill, too, deprecated severely the ways in which the powers of the unions were often used.

The same ambiguity persists into the neoclassical period. Marshall, who developed at some length a case for the inferior bargaining power of unorganised labour, who praised some aspects of the results of the rise of trade unionism and who had many friendships among the trade-union leaders of his day, could not have been more emphatic about the dangers of restrictive practices. Writing to the Master of Balliol *apropos* of the engineers' strike of 1897, he went so far as to say that 'Unless the A.S.E. *bona fide* concedes to the employers the right to put a single man to work on an easy machine, or even two or more of them, the progress of the English working classes from the position of hewers of wood and drawers of water, to masters of nature's forces, will, I believe, receive a lasting check. If the men should win, and I were an engineering employer, I would sell my works for anything I could get and emigrate to America.'* But a little later it was the Liberal Party which certainly claimed, rightly or wrongly, some connection with Classical Liberalism, that promoted the Trade Disputes Act of 1906 which conferred immunity on the funds of trade unions for damages for torts committed in the course of industrial action and created anomalies which have not yet been eliminated. And I would say that, for a long time after that, there was a certain constraint, not to say mealy-mouthedness, about the pronouncements of many professional economists on such matters.

I doubt, however, if unequivocal support of monopoly in the labour market would be characteristic of the attitude of the majority of Liberal economists today. The feeble associaations which aroused the sympathies of men of goodwill in the first half of the nineteenth century have grown into formidable combinations exerting considerable power both in the detailed and general evolution of economies; and the verdict of non-partisan analysis must be much more discriminating.

Let me say at once that I have no doubt of the benefits which, in the past, the existence of trade unions has often brought to

*Memorials of Alfred Marshall, ed. A. C. Pigou (London: Macmillan, 1925) p. 398. The letters to Bishop Westcott in the same collection (pp. 383–97) on the subject of trade unions are very revealing.

the working classes, at any rate in the United Kingdom. I do not believe that, up to a short time ago, they were able substantially to raise wages in general above the level which otherwise they would have attained; the verdict of statistical history, I think, points strongly to that conclusion. But that they were able to redeem special groups of persons from unjust treatment, that they were able to secure improvements in the law, not detrimental to the general interest and beneficial to the workers, that they have provided a background of self-respect and a training for statesmanship amongst the working classes in general, these are propositions which, I suppose, few detached observers of U.K. conditions would wish to contest.

Nevertheless there is a debit side also to the account. As I have just said I do not believe that until quite recently the existence of trade unions had much effect on the general level of wages. But in particular areas, where the trade unions concerned had tight control of recruitment, the possibilities were otherwise, and substantial monopoly gains accrued to persons in the groups in question while, at the same time, those who were excluded had to work elsewhere at lower margins. The high rates prevailing in the printing of London newspapers is an obvious example. The exclusion of women from many forms of activity in which they have no physical disadvantage is a wider instance of the same sort of consequence. So is the position of coloured labour in areas where white trade unions exercise exclusive power.

Assessment of the effects of strikes organised by trade unions presents complex problems. Speaking broadly of conditions prevailing until comparatively recent times, I am inclined to think that they can be exaggerated. Given a fairly inelastic money supply and the absence of the kind of indirect support from welfare services which has arisen in the last quarter of the century, it is arguable that the effect of most strikes was to bring about, somewhat more quickly, changes which were already on the way. And certainly, although the time lost by strikes must have been damaging to production, it was usually likely to be less damaging than the common estimate.

Much more serious in my judgement, so far as the rate of growth of the economy is concerned, has been the effect of restrictive practices, demarcation of areas of operation, limitation on freedom of entry, and so on. I have no doubt whatever that cumulatively these can be a very severe drag on industrial efficiency; they certainly are so in the United Kingdom where, in many industries, if such impediments to the economical deployment of labour were to vanish, there could be almost immediately a virtually discontinuous jump in the rate of output, and the rate of future progress could be much greater.

How to deal with the problems arising from the existence of such monopolies as trade unions is a problem not only of great practical but also of great intellectual and philosophical difficulty. That the general case for liberty includes liberty of association is not in question; there is no support for the *Loi de Chapellier* nowadays. The question here, as with other forms of liberty, is what to do when liberty for the individual, or group of individuals, involves encroachment on the liberties of others outside the group. And here, too, surely the general answer must be that, in such cases, there must be superior control. The liberty of each individual or group of individuals must be restrained within limits which prevent such encroachments. A framework of law for all is a precondition of the existence of liberty for each.

Stated thus, the principle is not difficult to accept for any who subscribe to the general desirability of liberty. The difficulties arise in the application to particular areas; and they are particularly acute in the region of association for more than one purpose, which is certainly often the case with trade unions with their traditions of provision of relief, legal aid and the negotiating skill in collective bargaining for their members, services which need not in the least involve monopoly and restrictive practice. Such difficulties may be freely admitted, as may those arising from less rational considerations of group solidarity – it is often unwise to attempt to change entire historical situations overnight. But recognition of all such problems does not imply admission of the claim to exemption from the rule of law such as has often been made on behalf of trade unions. This is a counsel of complete despair: where unjustifiable power exists, it is folly to suppose that it will never be exercised. Thus in the conditions in which most Western communities find themselves at present, I see no reason why particular types of association of producers which take the form of the modern trade union or professional association should not come within the ambit of the general legal structure deemed appropriate for the control of monopolies and monopolistic practices. Judged from the purely quantitative point of view there can be little doubt that monopoly in these areas does far more harm in the modern world than almost anywhere else. Doubtless there are special problems in this connection which need special consideration and special solutions. But the general contention that trade unions, equally with other associations, should be subject to the rule of law and that the branch of law which is applicable is that relating to monopoly and monopolistic practices in general seems to me to be intellectually and morally irrefutable.

In recent years the existence of trade unions and collective bargaining has given rise to new problems. Given a financial system which is reasonably stable, what I have said already indicates the main areas in which internal disharmonies can arise. If, however, there exists great elasticity of money and credit, if aggregate expenditure is not subject to limitation, either for reasons of deliberate policy or as a result of the inner logic of the system, then new possibilities present themselves; and the influence of the results of collective bargaining may be very serious indeed – prices and incomes chasing one another in an inflationary spiral highly inimical to the stability both of the economic process and social relationships in general. But this is a topic with which it is more appropriate to deal in the wider context of the subject of the next two chapters.

CHAPTER 5

The Stability of the System as a Whole

THE NATURE OF THE PROBLEM

The Classical conception of a System of Economic Freedom, which I have been discussing in the preceding chapters, clearly rested on an important assumption, namely that, in the long run at any rate, available resources would be reasonably fully employed. I say *in the long run* for I do not believe that any competent Classical Economist would have urged that, if there were sudden or large changes in demand, there would be an instant response; whatever may be said by those who have never read them with any attention, the members of that school were not unaware that shifts took time. I say also *reasonably* fully employed. Again I do not think that any Classical Economist would have expected that, in conditions subject to incessant change of seasons of technique and taste, there would be an unemployed percentage – of zero – or something only very narrowly removed from zero, as has occurred in more than one area in the period of inflationary pressure since the Second World War.

Now this assumption is not self-evident. The records of most modern economies do indeed show that, save in conditions of acute deflation, the vast majority of would-be workers in fact have been employed. In the years for which statistics are available, until the depression of the 1920s and 1930s in this century, U.K. employment figures seem to have been very seldom below 90 per cent and usually much above. This may indeed be held to afford some presumption that beliefs in a long-run tendency to reasonably high employment were not misplaced. Nevertheless the fact that between the upper and lower percentages there were ups and downs certainly constituted an intellectual problem, even if, as we shall see, there was – and is – no fool-proof policy in sight for dealing with it. And, needless to say, both deflation and inflation on a large scale, the result of governmental policies, create additional problems of their own.

THE SO-CALLED LAW OF MARKETS

Unfortunately, at the very outset, discussion of such matters was more than usually confused by the controversy whether lapses from reasonably brisk trade were due to partial or to general overproduction. J. B. Say, James Mill and David Ricardo were apprehensive of the frequently held view that, if any demand were displaced, there would be no alternative uses for productive resources. They therefore insisted that, in the nature of things, there could be no general glut and that all disturbances of trade were due to disproportionate investment. In his proposition that 'what is annually saved is as regularly consumed as what is annually spent',*Adam Smith had argued as if all savings were regularly invested – a view which excluded the likelihood of changes in the propensity to hoard. To this, James Mill and Say – the latter with reservations often overlooked – had added variations of what Say had called the Law of Markets, the assertion that the fact that the process of production produced incomes meant that, in the aggregate, supply created its own demand. As James Mill put it, 'Demand and supply are terms which are related in a peculiar manner. A commodity which is supplied, is always, at the same time a commodity which is the instrument of demand. A commodity which is the instrument of demand is always at the same time, a commodity added to the stock of supply. Every commodity is always, at one and the same time, matter of demand and matter of supply. . . . But if the demand and supply of every individual are always equal to one another, the demand and supply of all the individuals in the nation, taken aggregately, must be equal. . . . The demonstration therefore is complete.'† General overproduction

---

Wealth of Nations, vol. 1, p. 320.
†*Elements of Political Economy,* 3rd edn (1844) pp. 232–3.

therefore was ruled out. If there were an excess of supply in one branch of production, there must be a corresponding excess of demand somewhere else.*

This analysis, not unnaturally, did not carry conviction to all who encountered it, especially to any who had some eye to what was going on around them at the time – the catastrophic depression following the end of the Napoleonic wars. Malthus wrote that,

> The stagnation which has been so generally felt and complained of since the war appears to me inexplicable upon the principles of those who think that the power of production is the only element of wealth, and who consequently infer that if the powers of production be increased, wealth will certainly increase in proportion. Now it is unquestionable that the powers of production were increased by the cessation of war, and that more people and more capital were ready to be employed in productive labour; but notwithstanding this obvious increase in the powers of production, we hear everywhere of difficulties and distresses, instead of ease and plenty. . . . It is generally said that there has not been time to transfer capital from the employment where it is redundant to those where it is deficient. But I cannot persuade myself that this transfer can require so much time as has now elapsed since the war; and I would again ask, where are the understocked employments, which according to this theory ought to be numerous and fully capable of absorbing all the redundant capital, which is confessedly glutting the markets of Europe in so many branches of trade?†

As is well known, Malthus's diagnosis of the trouble was an excess of saving and a deficiency of consumption, which at first sight seems similar to the analysis developed in recent years; and, indeed, so it seemed to Keynes who hailed it as an anticipator of his own work. Unfortunately for this interpretation it is based on misconception. In Malthus's terminology 'saving' is equivalent to 'investment' in the modern sense of the word;

---

*As indicated above, Say, with whose name the cruder forms of this conclusion are often associated, in fact was much more cautious than the British exponents. For a useful analysis of what he actually said, see T. Stowell, *Say's Law* (Princeton University Press, 1972).

†*Principles of Political Economy* (1820) pp. 498–9.

he goes out of his way to deny that increased saving can take the form of an increased propensity to spend. 'No political economist of the present day,' he said, 'can by saving mean mere hoarding; and beyond this contracted and inefficient proceeding, no use of the terms in reference to national wealth can well be imagined, but that which must arise from *a different application of what is saved* [my italics] founded upon a real distinction between the different kinds of labour which may be maintained by it.* So he, and most of his fellow under-consumptionists, were debarred from the only conception, the conception of savings running to waste, which would have made plausible this argument. If diminished consumption meant an equivalent increase in investment, there was no reason to suppose any diminution in aggregate expenditure.

Thus arose the paradoxical position of orthodoxy arguing that no general glut was conceivable and Malthus pointing to the obvious existence of such a state of affairs but denying the conceptual means whereby this could be logically explained.

This situation was an anxiety to John Stuart Mill. He wrote to a friend that, in an article which this friend was writing, he should 'avoid the phrase "glut" or any other which will bring you into seeming collision (though not real) with my father's and Say's doctrine respecting a general glut. It may easily be shown that they were right; and yet Chalmers and Wakefield are not wrong.'†

Eventually he made just such an attempt in the remarkable paper on 'The Influence of Consumption on Production' written probably in the late 1820s or early 1830s but published much later in the mid-1840s in his *Essays on Some Unsettled Questions of Political Economy*.‡ In this paper, while insisting that in general and in the long run what is needed for economic growth is increased production rather than increased consumption, he admits explicitly that 'In order to render the argument for the impossibility of an excess of all commodities

---

*T. R. Malthus, *Principles of Political Economy* (1836) p. 32. Chalmers and Wakefield may broadly be described as taking the same line as Malthus in this respect.

† *The Earlier Letters of John Stuart Mill*, ed. Francis E. Mineka (Toronto University Press, 1963) p. 236.

‡Reprinted in *Essays on Economics and Society*, ed. J. M. Robson (Toronto University Press, 1967) pp. 262–79.

applicable to the case in which a circulating medium is employed, *money must itself be considered as a commodity* [my italics]. It must, undoubtedly be admitted that there cannot be an excess of all other commodities, and an excess of money at the same time.'

This certainly saves the formal position for the so-called Law of Markets but only at the expense of sacrificing its applicability to the explanation of what was in question in the arguments about the real world. As he goes on to say,

> those who have, at periods such as we have described, affirmed that there was an excess of all commodities, never pretended that money was one of these commodities; they held that there was not an excess, but a deficiency of the circulating medium. What they called a general superabundance, was not a superabundance of commodities relatively to commodities, but a superabundance of all commodities relatively to money. What it amounted to was, that persons in general, at that particular time, from a general expectation of being called upon to meet sudden demands, liked better to possess money than any other commodity. Money, consequently, was in request, and all other commodities were in comparative disrepute. In extreme cases money is collected in masses, and hoarded; in the milder cases, people merely defer parting with their money, or coming under any new engagements to part with it. But the result is that all commodities fall in price, or become unsaleable. When this happens to one single commodity, there is said to be a superabundance of that commodity; and if that be a proper expression, there would seem to be in the nature of the case no particular impropriety in saying that there is a superabundance of all or most commodities, when all or most of them are in this same predicament.*

It is clear from the rest of the argument that Mill regarded this possibility of an excess demand for money, or as some nowadays would care to put it an adverse gap between planned saving and planned investment, as being essentially a short-term phenomenon, whereas pessimists, fearing, in the absence of

*Ibid. p. 271.

new inventions, the nearness of a zero rate of return to accumulation, might have argued that it could persist for longer periods. But at least the bar to the consideration of such possibilities imposed, or supposed to be imposed, by the Law of Markets was removed.*

In their valuable survey of modern controversy regarding Say's Law and so on Messrs Baumol and Becker say of this paper that if one reads it today 'one is led to wonder why so much of the subsequent literature had to be written at all'.† This, I think, is true. But it also true that in his *Principles* Mill, himself, although to the seeing eye taking care to use terminology permitting the possibilities revealed by the earlier article, never really brings them out into the open. Still less

---

*It is interesting to observe that much the same solution had been put forward by Torrens in his *Essay on the Production of Wealth* (1821). On pp. 419–22 he says 'In all ordinary states of the market, prices will be determined by the proportion which exists between the quantity of commodities to be circulated and the amount of the currency with which their circulation is effected; and to occasion a general fall or rise of prices, the quantity of commodities must increase or diminish, while the amount of currency remains the same, or the amount of currency must increase or diminish, while the quantity of commodities remains the same. In periods of glut and general stagnation, however, prices are determined by other circumstances, and the exchangeable power of money will increase in a much higher ratio than the quantity of commodities. The reason is obvious. Money being the universal equivalent and medium of exchange, whoever can command a sufficient quantity of it, can immediately procure all the other articles he may desire to possess. Hence, that want of due proportion between the quantities of the several things produced and brought to market, which renders it difficult to exchange commodities against commodities, never can render it difficult to exchange money against commodities. A redundant harvest, which rendered it difficult for the farmer to exchange his corn for clothing, would interpose no difficulty in the way of exchanging his money for clothing. The farmer, therefore, who wished to replace that portion of his capital which consisted in clothing, would seek in the first instance, to convert his corn into money; while the manufacturer of clothing, though he might have obtained as much corn as he was able to consume, and as much sugar and tobacco, ribbons and lace, as he wished to consume, would nevertheless be desirous of turning his stock into money; because money being the universal equivalent, and imperishable in its nature, would be more useful to him than clothing in effecting future purchases when he required a fresh supply of corn, or of luxuries. Hence on every occasion of glut or general stagnation, the desire of turning goods into money is rendered more intense than the desire of turning money into goods, and the proportion in which prices will fall, will be much greater than that in which the relation between the quantity of commodities and the amount of currency will be altered.' The essential sentences in this passage are quoted in my *Robert Torrens and the Evolution of Classical Economics* (London: Macmillan, 1958) p. 286.

†'The Classical Monetary Theory: The Outcome of the Discussion', *Economica*, XIX (Nov 1952) pp. 335–7.

does he emphasise the limited applicability of his father's dogmatism. And although thenceforward, as in Marshall's well-known description of depression, fluctuations of confidence certainly play their part,* the full development of the analysis which Mill's insight made possible did not take place until comparatively recent times.

METAL *VERSUS* PAPER

All this discussion had singularly little influence on questions of policy. From the point of view of its supporters, the so-called Law of Markets was a useful debating point against arguments for protection and such-like pleas. But as regards the stability of the system as a whole, it led to a negative attitude and, in the post-Napoleonic war deflation, to a degree of blindness to the true state of affairs which is a blot on the record of the out-standing men who believed it.† As for the opposing under-consumptionist views, for the most part they were singularly lacking in positive proposals. Malthus was laodicean even about public expenditure.‡ Lauderdale, indeed, produced arguments against the repayment of debt by sinking funds which were the nearest he got to a glimmering of modern ways of posing the problem.§ The most important propaganda to come from this stable was Wakefield's proposals for colonisation¶ which, incidentally, invoked under-consumption at home and, which, as we have seen, were in John Stuart Mill's mind in his attempted reconciliation.

It must not be thought, however, that the main tradition of Political Economy in the Classical period was indifferent to questions of over-all stability: the leading exponents of this

*Alfred and Mary Paley Marshall, *The Economics of Industry* (1879) pp. 154-5. This is quoted by D. H. Robertson, *Lectures on Economic Principles* (London: Staples Press, 1959) vol. III, pp. 200-1, and in my *Theory of Economic Development*, pp. 65-6.

†See, for instance John Stuart Mill's review of Blake's *Observations on the Effects produced by the Expenditure of Government during the Restriction of Cash Payments* (1823) reprinted in J. S. Mill's *Essays on Economics and Society*, pp. 1-22. This antedates the famous *Essay on the Influence of Consumption on Production* discussed above.

‡See his letter to Ricardo on 2 Jan, 1817, Ricardo's *Works*, ed. Sraffa, vol. XI, pp. x-xi.

§See the interesting analysis of his position in Professor Corry's 'Lauderdale and Public Debt – A Reconsideration', in *Essays in Honour of Lord Robbins*, ed. Maurice Peston and Bernard Corry (London: Weidenfeld & Nicolson, 1972) pp. 151-9.

¶See his *England and America* (1833) especially pp. 107-34.

tradition were indeed very interested, as the volume of the literature bears witness. But the focus of their interest lay not primarily in the sphere of output and employment but in the sphere of money and credit, a sphere in which there was seldom any question of the existence of some positive functions of government. The problem was not whether in some sense or other the state was responsible for the integrity of money, but rather what such responsibilities were.

In the period when the main development of Classical monetary theory took place, the leading question was the relative preferability of metal or paper as a basis for the monetary system. At earlier times the existence of a metallic basis had been more or less taken for granted. As far back as Aristotle the desirability of a medium of exchange had received theoretical justification; and the advantages of the precious metals in this role had been set forth and reproduced again and again since then. In due course of time, credit instruments made their appearance and played their part in the settlement of accounts. But, while, as we know, David Hume perceived the disequilibrating role they might play, the desirability of their immediate convertibility was assumed almost without argument and any departures from this rule, as in the case of certain American colonial currencies alluded to by Adam Smith, were regarded as aberrations to be mentioned only to be deprecated. Law's famous proposal to issue money on the strength of land values had been rejected by the Scottish Parliament; and the subsequent débâcle of his conduct of the French finances only served further to discredit any such notions.

But now the disturbances following the French Revolution and the Napoleonic wars had posed the question of metal *versus* paper as a very serious issue. The suspension of cash payments of 1797 had been justified *ad hoc* as a prevention of a catastrophic run on the banks: it was so defended by Baring* and Thornton, but it had left the economic life of Great Britain with an inconvertible paper currency with a strong tendency to inflation and depreciated exchanges. The practical problems therefore were, was this state of affairs to be allowed to continue, and, if not, how was it to be brought to an end?

*Francis Baring, *Observations on . . . the Bank of England and the Paper Circulation* (1797) pp. 61 ff.

To the first of these questions the Classical answer was decidedly no. There were some differences among members of this group concerning the degree to which the rise of prices and the depreciation of the exchanges were due to causes other than the paper inflation: but all agreed that some at any rate had this origin; and, having reached this conclusion, which has its classic formulation in the famous Report on *The High Price of Gold Bullion* (1810), they recommended strongly against the continuation of paper as a base.

In commenting on this attitude, Jacob Viner, whose knowledge of the relevant literature was probably without rival, remarked that he had not been able to find any serious attempt during this period to meet the claims sometimes made by anti-bullionists that a currency standard better than metal was available.* This, I suspect, is true. But in judging this attitude it should be remembered – what, alas, is still true today – that in spite of some deterioration in the value of money based upon metal, the experience of the world with paper had been much worse. The catastrophe of the French *assignats* was still fresh in men's minds; and the conduct of the Bank of England when free from the obligation of convertibility had been such as to make Henry Thorton who, in his *Paper Credit* had been one of its defenders,† into one of its severest critics. When Ricardo, testifying before the Commons Committee of 1819 that a currency less variable than a metallic standard could not be attained by any system that he had 'ever even imagined',‡ he was not arguing without strong practical justification.

Unfortunately there is less to be said for the record of the Classical writers on the answer to the second part of the question, that is if metal was to be preferred, how was the return to be managed? Clearly the recommendation of the Bullion Committee that cash payments should be resumed while the war was at its height was not very sensible. But leaving that on one side and assuming less anxiety as regards international political relations, there remained the very important question *at what rate* was the return to convertibility

---

*See his *Studies in the Theory of International Trade* (New York: Kelley, 1937) p. 214.
†Henry Thornton, *Paper Credit* (1802) pp. 64–7.
‡Ricardo, *Works*, ed. Sraffa, vol. v, p. 388.

to be engineered. Since suspension there had been a considerable inflation. In the absence of a parallel movement elsewhere – which was improbable – to resume metallic payments at the old parity involved a considerable internal deflation with all the depressing consequences which such a contraction must carry with it.

Thanks to the researches of Mr Sraffa, we now know that in 1811, in order to prevent further inflation, Ricardo himself was prepared to countenance convertibility for a period at a depreciation of more than 20 per cent, although he went on to propose a gradual return to its former value.* We know too that much later in a letter to Wheatley he stated that he would not favour such a return if the disparity between the internal and external value of money was excessive.† But the fact remains that, in 1819, he himself misconceived just this relationship and supported the recommendation then made by the Committee of that date for a return to the old parity. Moreover, it must be admitted that, during the crushing deflation of 1815 onwards, the Classical writers and those under their influence exhibited no real awareness of the cause of the contemporary troubles alleging all sorts of explanations other than the obvious one of contraction of the circulation.‡ It is not to the Classical Economists but to those who subsequently – partly by their own fault – became regarded as currency – cranks, like the Attwoods, that we have to turn for the true explanation of what happened in those disastrous years.§ It was

*Ibid. vol. vi, pp. 67–80.
†Ibid. vol. ix, pp. 71–4.
‡Ibid. vol. v, p. 388.
§See, for example, Thomas Attwood's *Letters to the Earl of Liverpool on the question of the Bank Restrictions Act* (Birmingham, 1819) especially pp. 34–8. 'It is extraordinary also to observe the coolness with which the Committees speak about the Bank of England, and country bankers, having sufficient time "to call in their accommodations". One of the greatest evils of the division of labour is, that it so concentrates men's mind and habits upon particular objects of pursuit, that few people know anything at all beyond the range of those immediate objects; and this is the case of the two Committees. They know nothing at all of the business of banking. "To call in accommodation", may be sport to them, and to the bankers, but it is death to the public. I wish that the Committees were to spend twelve months in a banking house, during the period of a general "calling in of accommodations". They would get more knowledge of human life and of its ways and means, in that short period, than is to be learnt in all the books that ever were written from the beginning of the world. Nor would this "calling in of accommodations", be any very agreeable task to the Bankers, if they were all acting upon

not to the wickedness of employers, nor the introduction of machinery nor the deficiencies of the Poor Law that the widespread distress and unrest of this period was chiefly due: it was the deflation of credit. And it is greatly to be deplored that realisation of this was not more widely diffused in the present century when, after the First World War, a similar policy was adopted by the U.K. government with similarly unhappy results.

BIMETALLISM AND THE PRICE LEVEL

For something like a hundred years from the British restoration of cash payments in 1821, the issue of metal *versus* paper as an ultimate basis for monetary systems was, roughly speaking, dead. This is not to say that from time to time there did not occur proposals for what were sometimes called abstract systems; but these made little noise in the world. The business world was overwhelmingly in favour of a 'real' backing for currency and credit: and economists in general shared the belief that, with all their possibilities of fluctuations and their dependence on the accidents of geological discovery and mining technique, the precious metals afforded a securer basis for exchange and accounting than paper issued by governments.

This does not mean, however, that no attention was paid to the problem of possible changes in the value of such a basis. Once the fundamental decision had taken place, it is true that, for the next few decades, what had become the established position was taken more or less as *chose jugé*. But as the century wore on, apprehensions of a rate of increase in the stock of gold insufficient to maintain the trade without a deflationary drag on prices began to be prevalent. On the one hand, the value of silver was declining in relation to gold and there were strong tendencies for more and more national currencies to move on to a gold basis: on the other hand, the volume of

it at the same time. It would be very much like squeezing blood out of a stone. . . . There can indeed be no doubt that any private banker, who should be acting upon this system, whilst all other Bankers were asleep, would find it easy enough; but if all Bankers were to be acting upon it at the same time, they also would find their object recede before them as they advanced. They would find it utterly impossible "to call in their accommodations" from a languishing and exhausted country.'

transactions throughout the world was increasing. The decline in price levels after the beginning of the 1870s was thought by many to be an impediment to the satisfactory development of economic life in general.

There therefore arose in various quarters an agitation, which lasted for the better part of a quarter of a century, for the revival and extension of bimetallic systems. It was argued that if the area of issuing centres which were open to buy and sell gold and silver at a fixed ratio were enlarged, the relationship in the world market between these two metals could be maintained unchanged and the supplies available, as a basis for monetary systems, would be more adequate. In this contention it is almost needless to say that the silver interests were not inactive, nor were there lacking politicians anxious to cash in on a possible demonology – mankind being 'crucified on a cross of gold', and so on and so forth. But it is fair to say that more disinterested support was forthcoming from a substantial number, though by no means all, of the leading economists of the day; and a not negligible literature developed in its favour – the work of Babour being perhaps the most distinguished.* In this context, the bimetallic controversy, which is not intellectually so uninteresting as many people imagine, may be regarded as embodying the first widely discussed proposals for conscious control of the stability of economic life in the international sphere and, as such, deserves attention and respect.

In the end nothing happened. The discovery, in the mid-1890s, of the cyanide process for extracting gold from hitherto intractible ores, made commercially viable the vast resources of the Rand and thus led to a considerable increase in the output of that metal; and from then until the outbreak of the First World War, the tendency of prices was upwards. The practical call for a change of standard therefore died down – save, of course, from the silver interests; and it became realised that the intellectual foundations of the plea for change were not so powerful as at one time might have been thought. The idea that the fluctuations in value of two metals would always be less than those of one was itself not *a priori* convincing. But even supposing that there was some presumption that way, the

*David Babour, *The Theory of Bimetallism* (1886).

method of realising it was ill-conceived. To stabilise the ratio in which the two metals exchanged meant, in the last analysis, that one or other would set the pace; and although the extension of the area of the system would have clearly made easier its maintenance, in the long run, it would have proved unstable. As Alfred Marshall showed in his famous article in the *Contemporary Review* of March 1887,* there would only have been true bimetallism, in the sense of a system based upon the values of both metals, if the monetary units had been exchangeable for a fixed *combination* of quantities of gold and silver rather than amounts based upon a fixed *conversion ratio*. As Marshall himself said, it is easy in theory to see it extended beyond gold and silver to other selected durable goods thus forming the basis of a more general commodity money. But at the time it was conceived, it must have passed merely as a curiosum, ingenious enough, but lacking in practicability in the complex world of international economic relations. In the years immediately preceding the outbreak of the First World War in 1914, the ascendance of gold was seldom questioned.

THE CONTROL OF CREDIT

The choice of a metal as the medium of exchange does not exhaust the problem of management of the monetary system. The existence of substitutes for metallic cash in the form of convertible notes or cheque-drawing facilities clearly affects the potential volume of spending, and if the value of these instruments is to be kept at par with the value of the metallic base, there arise technical problems of considerable complexity. Should the reserves to be kept against liabilities of this sort be regulated by law or will the obligation to convert on demand on the part of banks be sufficient to maintain the requisite caution? For if it is not then there may arise intense financial difficulties, an over-issue of credit instruments leading to internal panic – a rush to convert notes and deposits into hard cash – and external drains of the ultimate metallic reserves arising from excessive developments of incomes and prices at home as compared with abroad. In the historic development of discussion of such matters the internal and external difficulties

*Reprinted in *Memorials of Alfred Marshall*, ed. Pigou, pp. 188–211.

were usually discussed together. But here I shall concentrate on the internal problem with only incidental references to international complications, leaving these to be dealt with separately in a later chapter.

Now at the time of the Bullion Controversy, it was commonly held that the obligation to convert bank notes into metal would be a sufficient safeguard against crises of this sort, whether external or internal, or as usually happened, a combination of both. If bankers were liable to give metal for this sort of paper, then it was urged that that obligation would make them pay attention to the security of their issues and thus obviate the danger of excessive expansion. There was therefore no regulation of the notes issued either by the Bank of England or the so-called 'country banks'.

But things did not turn out this way. Convertibility was restored. But, at intervals, crises involving both internal and external drains occurred, sometimes with appalling intensity. The Classical Economists were divided on this problem.* A powerful group headed by Overstone, George Ward Norman and Torrens – the so-called Currency School – argued that convertibility was not enough and that the remedy was to be found in a change of law bringing it about that there were to be no further increases in country bank issues and that, apart from a fixed fiduciary issue, all notes issued by the Bank of England were to be backed 100 per cent with gold. In this way they thought that the money supply would behave roughly as if it were wholly metallic and consequently that convertibility would be guaranteed. Their opponents headed by Tooke, Fullerton and Wilson – the so-called Banking School – argued that such an obligation would merely impede the power of the Bank to deal with crises and that the obligation to convert still would be sufficient if the Bank of England would keep larger reserves and be prepared to use more discretion in lending.

In this controversy the Currency School scored a practical victory: the Bank Act of 1844 which, apart from a small fiduciary issue, compelled a one-to-one relationship between notes and gold cover and so was a faithful reflection of their views and a rejection of the position of their opponents. And,

*For a more detailed account of the controversies involved see my *Robert Torrens and the Evolution of Classical Economics*, especially ch. IV.

in the in-fighting on the intellectual plane, their arguments, at their best, exhibit much more analytical subtlety and insight than those of their opponents. Tooke and Fullerton actually argued that over-issue of convertible notes was impossible. When this argument was examined, it proved to rest on the contention that if over-issue took place, the notes would flow back – the celebrated Principle of the Reflux. They argued, as, difficult as it may be to believe, certain economists still continue to argue, that the volume of the circulation depended on the level of prices rather than prices on the volume of the circulation – a contention which it was not difficult to query by reference to the effects of mining discoveries of the sixteenth century. And, as we shall see later, their belief that adverse movements of the balance of payments could always be looked after by payments out of what they called the 'hoards' implied policies highly inimical to the maintenance of fixed parities. There can be little doubt that, in regard to such matters, the Banking School failed to sustain their case.

Nevertheless the exponents of the Currency Theory were also guilty of grave error. With the exception of Torrens, they positively refused to include bank deposits in their conception of money. They regarded banking facilities simply as operating to diminish the demand for money proper, convertible notes and cash. They failed to perceive that, in regard to its potential effects on the value of money, the creation of credit by increased lending, whether payment was made by note or cheque, directly increased the supply of money in the wider sense.* In consequence, their model lacked one of its necessary ingredients if the influences operating on prices and activity

*The case of Torrens is peculiar. In his letter to Lord Melbourne (London, 1837) he explained clearly the grounds (which had already been perceived by Pennington) for regarding bank deposits as money; and he seems to have repeated this in a draft treatise on *Money Banks and International Exchange* which he submitted to Overstone in 1857. This submission elicited an almost hysterical response from Overstone: 'If you publish this to the world – you let loose upon us the Floodgates of Confusion – it will be the Deluge of Monetary Science.' (*The Correspondence of Lord Overstone*, ed. D. P. O'Brien (Cambridge University Press, 1971) vol. II, p. 715) and Torrens, in a somewhat sycophantic letter, abandoned the project; 'I throw Deposits to the dogs' (Ibid. p. 717). But in 1858, in an anonymous article in the *Edinburgh Review* for January 1858, he reproduced his earlier analysis. At the earlier stage he seems to have thought that regulation of notes alone would involve indirect regulation of credit on the assumption of conventional reserve ratios. But, when he wrote this last article, he was not so sure that this always happened.

were to be satisfactorily explained; and their practical prescriptions, which limited the regulation of the circulation to notes, left out of control what had already become the predominant feature of the volume of payments. If deposits were convertible, then the fact that notes had a nearly 100 per cent cover did not avert the danger of excessive expansion of circulation in the wider and more appropriate sense of the word.

As time went on this became fully evident. After 1844, on more than one occasion, the reserve in the Banking Department of the Bank of England became so low that the Bank Act had had to be suspended; and, even when this was not so, the belief that in the last resort this might be done served to prevent the extremes of panic. To the end of his life Overstone maintained that what had happened had nothing to do with the Bank Act. And in a sense, of course, this was true: it was not what the Bank Act did so much as what it did not do which was open to criticism – which was certainly not the attitude of the critics.

As a result of such experiences, however, it gradually became plain that if confidence were shaken, then the duty of the Bank of England as a lender of last resort differed markedly from that of other financial institutions and that, if the effective circulation was being depleted by a flight into cash, then it was its function to offset this tendency by lending freely.

This view was emphatically contested by bankers such as Hankey, who urged that the intention of the Act of 1844 in separating the Issue and the Banking Departments of the Bank of England was specifically in order to permit the Banking Department to pursue its operations as a normal banking business. 'The more the conduct of the Bank of England is made to assimilate to the conduct of every other well-managed Bank in the United Kingdom', he wrote, 'the better for the Bank and the better for the country at large'.*

Hankey was a true supporter of the principles of 1844. But the logic of the situation was against him; and it is no accident that it was Walter Bagehot whose remote, and, in my judgement, ill-conceived Utopia lay in a system of completely free banking, with his strong sense of the practical, should have

*Thomas Hankey, *The Principles of Banking* (London, 1887) p. 30.

given the *coup de grâce* to such contentions. In 1873 in his famous *Lombard Street* he argued that 'Theory suggests and experience proves that, in a panic the holders of the ultimate bank reserves (whether one bank or many) should lend to all that bring good securities quickly, freely and readily. By that policy they allay a panic; by every other policy they intensify it.' And again, 'Nothing, therefore can be more certain than that the Bank of England has in this respect no peculiar privilege; that it is simply in the position of a bank keeping the banking reserve of the country, that it must in time of panic do what all other similar banks must do; that in time of panic it must advance freely and vigorously to the public out of reserve.'*

By the last quarter of the century, therefore, the principle had been established that, to avert disaster at a time of financial panic, positive action on the part of those responsible for the reserve of the banking system was essential. That is to say that there could be no question of *laissez-faire* as regards the ultimate security of the credit system. The way was therefore prepared for the conceptions which were to be developed later of a wider responsibility on the part of such institutions for the stable evolution of the volume of the circulation as a whole.

---

*Lombard Street, new edn (London, 1919) p. 165.

CHAPTER 6

The Stability of the System as a Whole (continued)

THE EFFECTS OF WAR

It was the outbreak of the First World War in 1914 which constituted a watershed in the history of thought regarding the management of the stability of the economic system as a whole. It must not be thought that the ideas which have been dominant since then have no counterpart in the past: on the contrary there can be discovered in the literature precedents for almost everything. But, so far as practical policy was concerned, and the thought which had some influence on it, the contrast is very evident. Up to then the underlying assumption had been that the main areas of the world were on common metallic standards, gold or silver; and although practical problems still arose where the relations between the gold and silver areas were concerned, this did not give rise to extensive theoretical discussion or to recommendations other than such as were directed to securing a more universal link with gold. Thus, while it may perhaps be argued, historically, that the then existing gold standard was by no means a close approximation to the models of the textbooks, the fact remains that theoretical speculation in the main assumed a monetary system which was essentially international in character and that the practical maxims which governed the conduct of policy were largely concerned to maintain the necessary connections.

The coming of war, however, and with it the inevitable break-up of the monetary unity of the world – such as it was – put an end to all that. The various nations involved pursued independent financial policies. They resorted in greater or lesser degree to the printing press and inflationary borrowing; and, in consequence, they suffered falls in the internal and external values of their respective currencies. In many cases this continued after the war and took the form of hyper-inflations which, more even than the war itself, wrought havoc among those recipients of incomes which were not quickly adjustable and, conspicuously in Germany and Austria, went far to undermine the central elements of stability in the structure of society and to destroy the potentialities of resistance to the barbaric upheavals of the 1930s which brought about the Second World War.

At first the effect of this spectacle of disorder and disaster was to produce a strong desire to return to the comparatively stable conditions of the pre-war era. It is worth noting that this feeling was even shared by Keynes and indeed voiced, with character-istic emphasis, in an article contributed to the *Manchester Commercial Supplement* for April 1922 in which he said, 'I see no other solution of stabilization except this traditional solution – namely a gold standard in as many countries as possible.' But whether this was a sensible reaction or not, policy directed to achieving it was hopelessly bungled by the U.K. government and the Bank of England. The one opportunity for a compara-tively painless return to gold for the United Kingdom, which still in those days, together with the United States, led the world in matters of finance, was a restoration of convertibility of sterling at a devalued parity shortly after the war. That would have provided a landmark and example of stability in the contemporary world disorder. It might well have mitigated the impact of deflationary influences after the collapse of the short-lived post-war boom. But the authorities, flagrantly disregarding all the lessons of the post-Napoleonic depression and, accepting as wisdom the pitiful advice of Lord Cunliffe and his associates, committed themselves to a return to gold at the old parity. They thus inflicted on the U.K. economy, and those parts of the world influenced by the U.K. economy, years of damaging uncertainty before eventually, in 1925, restoring convertibility at an overvalued rate.

As all the world knows, this policy was a failure. The new parity was maintained for some years at the cost of further restrictive pressures. Then in 1931, with the additional strains of the world depression, it broke down altogether, bringing much greater chaos in many parts of the world; and, for the time being at least, wide indifference to the idea of an international monetary system. In this way, at that time any hope – if 'hope' is the appropriate word – of the restoration of international monetary relations based on a common metal disappeared. The net effect, therefore, was to turn men's minds to the problems of local stability; and, for a time at least, the problem of maintaining orderly relations between local currencies receded into the background.

This is vividly illustrated by an exchange of views between the aged Marshall and Keynes. In 1887, in the essay mentioned in the previous chapter, Marshall had written 'Every plan for regulating the supply of the currency, so that its value shall be constant, must, I think, be national and not international.' In December 1923, Keynes relates, 'after I had sent him my *Tract on Monetary Reform*, he wrote to me, "As years go on it seems to become ever clearer that there ought to be an international currency, and that the – in itself foolish – superstition that gold is the 'natural' representative of value has done excellent service. I have appointed myself amateur currency-medicines; but I cannot give myself even a tolerably good testimonial in that capacity. And I am soon to go away: but, if I have the opportunity, I shall ask newcomers to the celestial regions whether you have succeeded in finding a remedy for currency maladies." ' Keynes added – in 1925 – '*As regards the choice between the advantages of a national and of an international currency I think that what he wrote in 1887 was the truer word, and that a constant value-currency must be, in the first instance at least, a national currency.*'

Thus the assumption of contemporary speculation, as represented at that time by Keynes, had become one of greater elbow-room for local experiment.

THE OBJECTIVES OF NATIONAL POLICY

I shall discuss the implications of all this for international economic relations in a later chapter. From the point of view of my present objective, a survey of the general principles held to be applicable to an economic system as a whole, I shall restrict myself here to the consequences of the assumption of greater elbow-room.

At first the focus of thought was concentrated upon the possibilities of price stabilisation. As I indicated in the preceding chapter, the sophisticated, as distinct from the naïve and parrot-like, preference for metal had been that, for all its vicissitudes, it value was likely to remain more stable than the alternatives. Compared with all known examples of paper, the record of gold had been relatively good. The hope was now – somewhat in defiance of the experience of the post-war hyper-inflations – that this record could be transcended and that a managed currency, not dependent on the vagaries of geological and technical discovery, could do better; and that management of the local price level could at least help to eliminate the ups and downs of the margin of economic activity as a whole within which the system had tended to fluctuate.

As we have seen, the subject was not altogether new; the possibilities of reducing the destabilising influences of changes in the value of money had been among the preoccupations of the more intelligent advocates of bimetallism. But then the background was a choice between *metallic* standards and was subject to very practical limitations. Now such constraints were less obtrusively obvious and discussions of the ideal were less confined. Was the optimal system to be regarded as a constant level of the prices of consumer goods measured in terms of some agreed index with the rates of pay rising with productivity? Or was it to be found rather in a constant level of incomes with prices falling as productivity increased? The case for the former could be argued in terms of a certain margin for adjustments of relative rates of pay without recourse to such positively down-ward revisions in certain sections which might be necessary if the object were constant *average* incomes. An appealing case for the latter could be based upon the desirability of a state of affairs in which the recipients of fixed money incomes partici-pated in a general increase in productive power. There was even a school of thought – to which the present writer gave some adherence – which held that the objective of constant commodity prices might itself be destabilising in that it might involve financial injections which distorted the investment structure, a possibility which was later held to have been sustained by the boom in the United States before 1929. It all seems a long time ago nowadays and, in any case, it was somewhat unreal when divorced from international complications. But there was a good deal of intellectual subtlety involved; and some at least of the issues have come to life again recently in discussions of financial policy in a wider context.

Then came the Great Depression of the 1930s, an event so catastrophic in its consequences on trade, production and employment as to raise in the minds of many the question whether the assumptions of the System of Economic Freedom had not shown deficiencies which were only to be remedied by a shift to Total Collectivism. This, I am clear, was a misapprehension. What had gone wrong was not the decentralised initiative of a system of free enterprise, but rather a degree of deflation of aggregate expenditure which made the calculations of such initiative erroneous and the conduct of enterprise unprofitable. But, even where this was recognised, there was involved a change of focus in the formulation of objectives. This is vividly exemplified in the contrast between Keynes's *Treatise on Money* and his *General Theory*. In the former work the emphasis was on stabilisation of *prices*; in the latter it was the stabilisation of *employment*. In the former the theoretical background was still the Quantity Theory of Money, in the latter the determinants of aggregate expenditure: the propensity to consume and the inducement to invest. Needless to say, where so able a thinker was concerned, it is important not to exaggerate the contrast. The Keynes of the *Treatise* was certainly concerned with the ups and downs of employment, as had been many of his predecessors for at least half a century. The Keynes of the *General Theory* would certainly not have denied the importance of preventing instability in the value of money once the tendency to underemployment had been corrected.* But the shift of preoccupations is unmistakable; and if this was true of Keynes, how much more so for public opinion in general.

As time went on, preoccupation with employment in the

---

*In any full assessment of Keynes's attitude, consideration of the emphasis of the *General Theory* must be conjoined with that of the pamphlet issued shortly after the outbreak of the hostilities, *How to Pay for the War* (London: Macmillan, 1940). The reaction against the naïvities of some of Keynes's followers is grossly unjust, if it accuses Keynes himself of ignoring the dangers of inflation.

criterion of the success of the control of the aggregate system was reinforced by two further circumstances.

First, the results of rearmament and war expenditure. As this developed in the United Kingdom, what had seemed to be chronic underemployment diminished at a brisk rate until, when the war mobilisation was in full swing, unemployment was virtually non-existent. Later on the same development took place in the United States. Little wonder that it was felt that if governments possessed this power of preventing the horrors of the early 1930s they should be prepared to use it.

Added to this, it must be realised that, at that time, it was widely anticipated that once the war was over, after perhaps a brief flare-up in the commodity markets, investment would once more flag and the world lapse into depression. Keynes himself can be not unfairly described as a 'stagnationist' in the sense that he found it difficult to believe that the propensity to invest, if unaided, was likely for long to remain above what he would have regarded as a danger point for reasonably active use of resources; and this attitude was widely diffused among high authorities in the United States – conspicuously Alvin Hanson. The days of the frontier were over, it was contended, the probability of inventions, which would offer rates of return likely to evoke a disposition to invest nearly approaching the disposition to save, was remote. The efforts of men of goodwill therefore should be so to shape national and international institutions as to provide suitable safeguards against *de*flation. Any fear of *in*flationary influences was entertained only by a very restricted minority.

THE AMBIGUITIES OF EMPLOYMENT POLICY

In such circumstances it was not unnatural that the avoidance of economic depression and the maintenance of high levels of employment should become declared objectives of policy. The Coalition Government in the United Kingdom set the example during the war with a special White Paper; and thereafter many states committed themselves in one way or another to the same aim. There was, moreover, much public discussion. Sir

D

William Beveridge (afterwards Lord Beveridge), a great expert on social insurance in general, produced a book described as a 'Report' – as if it were a government document (which it was not) – entitled *Full Employment in a Free Society** which, in promises and policy, went well beyond the carefully guarded phrases of the Coalition Government's White Paper. It may well be regarded as archetypal of the mood in which much educated opinion contemplated the problems of the future.

Unfortunately, as is apt to happen with blanket pronouncements and promises of this sort, there were important omissions and ambiguities which went far to confuse expectations in this respect.

First come ambiguities as regards measurement. It is of course a sign of pure ignorance or charlatanry to suggest that 'full employment', conceived in a general way as a desirable state of affairs, is a conception which only came into vogue some time in the 1930s. The earlier literature from Petty onwards affords plentiful examples of its use in just that sense. The Classical Economists may have assumed too readily that the financial and industrial systems of the day had inbuilt tendencies eventually to create such a condition whatever the occasion of disturbance. But one would have to look elsewhere to discover any belief that, for some reason or other, it was not desirable.

The difficulty which I am discussing arises when a further degree of precision is attempted. Quite obviously, in any society liable to internal or external change, 'full employment' does not mean that 100 per cent of the labour force is at work. At any moment, when a count is taken of the persons who are not at work, on any sensible definition there will be a certain number who will be moving from one job to another because of changes in the fundamental conditions of demand and supply; there will be some who are temporarily unemployed because of seasonal influences; there will be some who are not offering their services because the price which is being offered is unacceptable. Because of these complications the Coalition White Paper referred always to 'high levels of employment' rather than the easily misunderstood 'full employment'. Even

Full Employment in a Free Society, 2nd edn (London: Hillary, 1960).

Beveridge, who popularised the use of the term and made very far-reaching claims concerning the effectiveness of the policies he recommended, had a chapter devoted to showing that 'full employment' was not full employment in the zero-unemployment sense. Indeed the most he promised was an average unemployment of 3 per cent; so that since, even in the best regulated system, there must be some ups and downs, the actual figure would be sometimes more than 3 per cent and sometimes less. In fact, as is well known, for the greater part of the period since the war, in this country the unemployment percentage has been considerably less than 3 per cent – so much so that the general public, encouraged almost universally by politicians and the press, have come to expect anything approaching the Beveridgean norm as almost an indication of disaster. In an age of creeping and eventually accelerating inflation, this has certainly not made the conduct of policy any easier.*

The second ambiguity is even more serious: a blanket guarantee of 'full employment' without any reference to the relation of incomes and productivity can easily run into grave difficulty. It is reasonable, and indeed highly desirable, other things being equal, to try to make good a deficiency of aggregate demand which, with incomes rising *pari passu* with productivity per head, involves a slack use of resources. But if stability or near stability in the value of money is a desideratum, *it is not reasonable to undertake to provide 'full employment', whatever the relation of the rise in incomes demanded to the rate of increase of productivity.* Suppose, for instance, that productivity per head is rising at, say, 4 per cent per annum and there are demands for rises of pay averaging, say, 20 per cent. It is surely abundantly clear that, in such conditions, 'full employment' could only be maintained by increases in the volume of expenditure financed by inflation of one kind or another. It can be confidently asserted that the outlook of the Coalition White Paper contemplated no guarantee of high levels of employment in such circumstances; and although we know that policies have been

*Some of the difficulty certainly is attributable to the habit of quoting crude percentages of unemployment without any reference to the durations involved. An unemployment percentage of one, if it involved years out of work for the persons concerned, would be a serious social problem. A percentage of, say, five, if the duration of unemployment while changing jobs was a matter of weeks, would not be a matter of grave concern.

adopted which have had more or less this kind of result, it is difficult to believe that any government, however incompetent, would consciously give an assurance that, whatever rate of pay is demanded, sufficient purchasing power will be created to bring it about that 'full employment' is maintained. It is quite possible that, for a time at least, a substantial proportion of an electorate might prefer 'full employment' to comparative stability in prices. But experience suggests that a point must be reached eventually when this preference is reversed and policies designed to prevent complete collapse of the purchasing power of money assume priority.

THE INSTRUMENTS OF POLICY

The change in objectives as regards the stability of the system as a whole, which I have just traced, was paralleled by a change in conceptions of appropriate instruments.

Up to 1931, with the exception of the war period, the major instruments of policy were bank rate and informal management of credit, the objectives being limited to the maintenance of external equilibrium and the management of the gilt-edged market so as to secure rates of interest as favourable as possible to whatever government was in power. The use of fiscal policy to influence the tempo of economic activity as a whole, although occasionally the subject of public discussion, had certainly not loomed on the horizon as a policy likely to be adopted. The balanced budget, although not always achieved, was an animal sacred to most practical politicians – I say this as pure description, not with any desire at this stage to prejudge the issue.

The suspension of the convertibility of the pound in 1931 must be regarded as the beginning of change in this connection. The freeing of the pound and the sterling area from the fixed tie to gold gave a sense of increased freedom of manoeuvre as regards internal policy; and, although this was officially exploited chiefly in a gigantic conversion operation, a very substantial section of public opinion, of which I regret to say I was not one, argued that more might be done by way of public expenditure to relieve the effects of the depression on employment. At a later stage what was done – or thought to be done – in the United States,* reinforced this school of thought; and the spectacular effects of rearmament expenditure, to which I have alluded already, had a still further effect on men's minds. Thus, by the time of the issue of the Coalition White Paper, not to mention the Beveridge 'Report', it is no exaggeration to say that the conception of stabilisation by fiscal policy was almost completely in the ascendant.†

Conceptions of the appropriate techniques involved in this respect were the subject of some evolution. The idea of manipulating necessary public investment in the shape of roads, schools, hospitals and so on had been ventilated by Arthur Bowley as early as the Poor Law Commission of 1909; and, at the time of the 1929 election, Keynes and Henderson, in a widely read pamphlet issued on behalf of the Liberals entitled *Can Lloyd George Do It?*, elaborated it into a definite programme. Later on, Henderson who, probably on the strength of this, had been recruited by Ramsay MacDonald to act as secretary to the newly formed Economic Advisory Committee, lost his faith in this respect, largely, I imagine, because of what was perhaps too acute a perception of the administrative difficulties of timing this kind of expenditure; and he definitely repudiated his earlier propaganda. But Keynes was unconvinced by his retraction and, to the end, believed in the possibility of counter-

---

*The net effects of fiscal policy in the relief of depression in the United States during this period, and its comparative effectiveness when combined with the restrictive monetary policies of the Federal Reserve System, is still a matter of controversy. See especially Professor Milton Friedman's *Monetary History of the United States, 1867–1960* (Princeton University Press, 1963).

†An almost unbelievable but true story of an episode, witnessed by the present author at the press conference which released the Coalition White Paper, is an apt illustration of the extent to which thought on this subject had fallen into the background. The Editor of *The Economist*, at that time Geoffrey Crowther, slightly mischievously asked the high official representing the Treasury whether the absence of any very clear lead on monetary policy represented the abandonment of that instrument by the government. To this question, amazingly, the high official (now dead) replied, with emphasis, 'Oh no! not at all, when prices go up we shall put the Bank Rate down [sic] and when prices go down we shall put it up [sic].' It is only fair to the Treasury, that undeservedly much-abused institution, to add that the high official in question was not originally from that stable; it would have been quite inconceivable that, say Sir Richard Hopkins, or Sir Frederick Phillips, the leading intellects in that department during the war, would have answered in these terms. But what was said was certainly not just a slip of the tongue: the person who said it – a man who, at that time, bore very high responsibility in this respect – had not thought at all about monetary policy in general, let alone the relation between interest rates and price levels.

cyclical control of this sort* – as did an increasing volume of professional opinion at home and abroad.

Gradually, however, conceptions widened. If below-the-line capital expenditure might be so utilised, why not public expenditure in general? If the extreme pessimism of the school to which Henderson had given his adherence was not justified, nevertheless it was certainly true that the timing of public works of the kind envisaged presented difficulties in the procedures and delays of official investment. Thus, it came to be felt that it would be simpler just to abandon the objective of year-to-year balance in the ordinary budget and to use variations in expenditure and taxation as the main counter-cyclical instrument. There were divisions of opinion concerning safeguards in this respect. But, for a time, fiscal policy, either in the form of control of public investment or unbalancing or overbalancing the budget, dominated thought on general stabilisation.

Later on, again, conceptions became more eclectic. The revulsion against the use of monetary instruments which had reached its apogee in the preposterous episode of Dalton's attempt – at a time of great capital scarcity – to force the long-term rate of interest to a level of $2\frac{1}{2}$ per cent, began to wear off. In the United States the limitations on the room for manoeuvre of the Federal Reserve System impaired by the obligation to maintain the value of long-term government securities, produced a similar change of view. Early in the 1950s, therefore, the use of monetary policy as one of the instruments of stabilisation in the shape of Bank Rate and open-market operations, began once more to be admitted. Considerations of external equilibrium ensuing from international obligations also played a part.

By the middle of that decade this process had gone so far that there arose a demand for an official review of potentialities in

---

*I well remember his delight when, on the strength of investigations and calculations made by certain colleagues on an assumption of a multiplier of 2, I went along to his room one day and told him that 'by manipulating the more adaptable items in the public sector, it seemed as if variations of some £250 million might be possible at the then level of National income.' 'Exactly what I have always thought', I recollect him saying – I would not swear to the precise order of words – 'People think I am proposing something drastic when all that I think necessary is operations of this order of magnitude.'

this respect which resulted in the appointment of the *Radcliffe Committee on the Workings of the Monetary System*. In this connection the Report of this committee has two significant features. It admitted the possibilities of monetary measures as one of the instruments of stabilisation policy, though it deprecated undue expectations of their efficiency; and, in this connection, it focused attention on the relation between control of the liquidity of the system as a whole *via* the management of rates of interest. It tended to regard the supply of money as a consequence, rather than a determinant, of the achievement of the main objective. From the point of view of this essay, in spite of the high authority with which this argument was supported, it was not such as to clarify thought on the fundamental problem of methods of securing the stability of the system as a whole * I shall return to this matter later. But it is now time to turn to historical developments in the period under survey, that is the period since the revolution of objective and method from the end of the Second World War in 1945 up to the present day.

THE POST-WAR INFLATION

It cannot be said that history since the war has borne out the apprehensions from which the objectives of policy under discussion took their origin The problems of general stability with which the leading governments of the world have been confronted, have been *not* the prevention of unemployment and deflation but rather the reverse, overheating of the economy and inflation. Save for short intervals, explicable in terms of special causes, the level of employment in most industrial societies has been considerably higher than the average of previous periods; and, in some parts, the value of money has fallen at rates unprecedented save in wartime or the hyperinflations following the disorganisation of war. Certainly the United Kingdom has never known in peacetime rates of inflation such as have occurred in recent years.

Now some at least of the inflations of these years have been due to causes which have been well known in the past: govern-

*See my long analysis of the Radcliffe Report in my *Money, Trade and International Relations* (London: Macmillan, 1971).

ment expenditure not covered by revenue or non-inflationary borrowing, interest rates manifestly below any conceivable conception of equilibrium levels and the excess borrowing to which such facilities give rise. Demand inflation is not a new phenomenon. It has shown itself again and again in history. If there is anything new it is the intellectual climate in which it has taken place. It has been the fear of deflation, inherited from the 1930s, which has often inhibited governments from taking action to prevent it, lest they should be accused of policies inimical to employment and growth. The insistence of Beveridge that a policy of full employment involved a condition in which there were 'always more vacant jobs than unemployed men', that is a position in which the demand for labour was always in excess of supply, although he would have denied the reproach, was in fact a prescription for non-stop demand inflation.* But the general climate of public opinion tolerated such conceptions as if they were obvious good sense.

At the same time, during this period, there have developed influences on the cost side, which, although neither universal nor continuous, may also be said to have contributed to the process. If powerful groups of producers enjoying a monopoly demand increases of price or pay exceeding the value of their production at rates at which supply and demand have hitherto been in equilibrium, then one of two things must happen. Either there will be a falling off of demand for their products or, if the demand in that quarter is inelastic, for other people's products, and unemployment will follow; or, if fearing such an outcome and pledged to high levels of employment regardless of the effect on prices, governments or central banks create new purchasing power to sustain the markets, then there will be inflation. And if this gives rise to further demands elsewhere to maintain so-called relativities, then if, following the view that improved management can always bring it about that there can be an improvement of production commensurate with demands of any magnitude – a conclusion more appropriate to the nursery than to the real world – more matching purchasing power is provided, there will be further inflation, and so on.

This is the essence of the process of cost inflation. It can of

*See my critique of this work, 'Full Employment as an Objective', reprinted in my *Money, Trade and International Relations*, pp. 41–65.

course be argued – and argued with truth – that the ultimate condition of such demands leading to inflation, rather than unsold stocks and unemployment somewhere, is the creation of money to finance it. But it seems paradoxical to argue that the producers in question have *no* responsibility for what happens and that the *sole* cause of the inflation is the failure of the government to maintain a firm hold on the rate of increase of money supply. Such a policy is clearly a *necessary condition* for containing inflation. But in a *milieu* in which producers not increasing productivity per head by more than, say, 5 per cent per annum, demand increases of, say, 30 per cent in pay and if, at the same time, governments conceive themselves to be more or less pledged to maintain 'full employment' and are terrified by threats to essential supplies, to deny the part played by the original demands any entitlement to be described as contributing to the causal process seems a slightly fanciful – or politically ingenuous – approach to the explanation of what happens. It is the occurrence of sequences of this sort – call them what you will – which in an ealier chapter led me to argue that the increased power of the associations of producers in the modern world carried with it certain dangers and disadvantages not apparent in earlier periods.

The results of all this have followed much the same general pattern as the effects of other inflations at different times and different places. So far as internal effects are concerned, these can be grouped under three main headings. (It should be remembered that, throughout this argument, considerations of external complications are postponed, save in so far as they involve constraints and internal policy.)

First come distortions of the income structure. Persons and institutions whose money incomes are derived from contracts adjustable, if at all, only at infrequent intervals, suffer a diminution of real income absolutely and in comparison with those whose incomes vary with prices. This has two further consequences. Those with variable incomes tend to be much more alert in enforcing what they regard as appropriate variations: they are much more sensitive to relativities, much more careful not to fall behind the gun. At the same time those whose incomes are derived from ownership tend to shy away from fixed-interest investments; for the time being at any rate, there is a more than proportionate rise in equities and property of various kinds. This, in turn, gives rise to speculative activities rendering the whole structure considerably more vulnerable when the attempt is eventually made to arrest the inflationary process.

Secondly, there are far-reaching distortions in the organisation of production. At first profits improve and the prospects are rosy. But provision for future contingencies tends to be starved. Depreciation quotas continue to be based upon the assumption of a constant value of money. Thus when eventually, as a result of external apprehensions or internal disillusionment, interest rates rise to take some account of prospective falls in the purchasing power of money, the amounts set aside prove to be inadequate for replacement; and so liquidity difficulties emerge. In this way, as the inflation proceeds, there arises a need for further inflation to sustain existing levels of activity. Then, as public opinion hardens against the policies which give rise to such tendencies, bankruptcies and recession begin to show themselves.

Finally, there is a general tendency for a lowering of public and private morale. Inflation presents opportunities for quick gains. The casino-like atmosphere breeds a disregard of normal restraints – if *he* gets away with it, why shouldn't I? – and those who are left behind have a sense of grievance which itself involves a loosening of the social bond. This in turn leads to a highly discreditable competition among political parties to capitalise the discontents of bewildered and anxious people. To anyone who has an inkling of what it really happening the political scene becomes more and more unreal – and contemptible.

> Blest paper credit. Last and best supply
> To lend corruption lighter wings to fly.

So wrote Pope in the eighteenth century. How right he was of the third quarter of the twentieth.

PRICES AND INCOMES POLICIES

Confronted with developments of this sort, various governments have resorted to direct operations on prices and incomes. This has a certain initial appeal among those sections of the population not themselves affected: it smacks of no-nonsense action, strong government, a firm hand at the wheel and such-like affectively toned slogans; and, at a time of so-called crisis – usually induced by foreign-exchange difficulties – it may even command, for a time, more widespread support. But in the long run it is subject to certain quite important disadvantages.

As regards prices, while, as has been emphasised earlier, there can be no objection to regulation where natural or contrived monopolies are concerned, the effects of price control in general are apt to be deleterious. It is liable to widespread evasion: it is a matter of great difficulty for any administration, however efficient, to keep pace with changes in quality specification, conditions of sale and substitution of new products. Moreover, as all experience shows, the holding of prices below the level which equalises supply and demand, even in the absence of evasion, raises acute difficulties both on the demand and on the supply side of the market.

On the demand side it gives rise to 'shortages', queues, arbitrary privileges for special customers and eventually a demand for rationing in order to procure a fair distribution. On the supply side, if there is any short-run elasticity, there tends to be a diminution of replacements, a call for special subsidies, and so on. Thus, where so-called essentials are concerned, nothing less than thorough-going control from the centre is necessary if the 'shortage' on the demand side is not to be greatly worsened by a falling off of supply. In so far as it is successful, the repression of price inflation may have a short-term effect on the atmosphere of collective bargaining. But, in the end, it adds to the difficulty of controlling aggregate expenditure by reason of the accumulation of unspent balances.

As for the control of rates of pay, while there are certain short-run effects, to be discussed later, which may be favourable to the arrest of inflation, there can be little doubt of its disadvantages as a long-term policy. As with price control, it is an incentive to evasion – reclassification of jobs and arrangement of side-benefits become almost major branches of economic activit y where incomes policies prevail. It breeds the prevalence of an in tense sense of injustice. Some sections whose members feel that they have exceptional claims are bound to be left out by the imposition of the initial freeze; and it is unlikely that such grievances will be eliminated by more flexible administration later on. It is antipathetic to both employers and employed. Employers distrust it because it impairs their freedom of manoeuvre in the continual reorganisations which are the hallmark of efficient management. It is equally antipathetic to trade unions who feel that it deprives them of legitimate functions in collective bargaining and it imposes limitations on relativities which would emerge from the operation of the market. All experience hitherto suggests that in free societies controls of this sort, whatever their initial success, tend to crumble and eventually break down.

Such a conclusion, however, does not rule out the utility of such measures in certain special emergencies. If, for some reason or other, governments have eventually decided to deal with inflation by control of aggregate demand, a diminution of the rate of increase of money supply and a curb on public expenditure, then the degree of temporary unemployment which must inevitably be caused by such a policy will clearly be less if, for the time being, claims for increased incomes are at a standstill or less than they might otherwise have been. The case for an incomes policy – with perhaps some control of prices thrown in as a sweetener, irrational though that may be – rests therefore on its possible effect as an easement of the difficulties accompanying the cessation of financial inflation. It is essentially the case for an *emergency* rather than a *permanent* policy. But having regard to the fact that the majority of governments introducing prices and incomes policies usually think of them as substitutes for suitable financial measures, and indeed are often apt to conjoin then with renewed inflation – a dash for freedom, increased growth and such-like hollow clichés – such a case, although intellectually quite powerful, is liable to remain valid only as an academic possibility. The idea that, in a free society, the stability of the system as a whole is likely to be maintained by permanent prices and incomes policies to the total neglect of control of aggregate expenditure is surely an *ignis fatuus*.

A REFORMULATION OF OBJECTIVES

What then are we to think? What should be the objectives as regards stability of the system as a whole? And what are the methods available by which they should be attempted?

It must be remembered always that in this chapter we have been analysing the general principles of stabilisation as regards a closed system: the complications introduced by international economic relations have been deliberately postponed for later treatment. Bearing this in mind, we may approach the problems just posed by one generalisation which should be equally acceptable to all schools of thought, Keynesian or neoclassical, which accept stability as a *desideratum*, namely that aggregate expenditure should be so managed as to conform so far as possible to the value of aggregate output at a suitably chosen price level.

Now it is true that there may be some dispute about this. I leave out of account that school of thought which, regarding rapid growth *via* forced saving as the main objective of policy, has contended that inflation does not matter – that Latin American conditions are positively desirable if the rate of growth deemed desirable cannot be achieved any other way. There is really no arguing with this kind of irresponsibility. As I have indicated already I would treat with respect those whose optimal conditions were constancy of incomes with prices falling with increased productivity, though I should regard the implied condition as regards relative incomes – some falling, some rising – as on the severe side. Nor should I rule out the view that, having regard again to the problem of appropriate relativities, the position might be eased if the price level were allowed to rise slightly, say 1 per cent per annum. But as an intelligible and not necessarily impracticable objective, I prefer the norm already postulated of aggregate expenditure equivalent to the value of output at constant prices.

But, if this is adopted, what happens to employment policy? Are the undertakings given in the past to be ruthlessly thrown overboard? Not at all. There is nothing in what has just been said to negate the policy of endeavouring to avoid unemployment due to positive deflation. On the contrary, it is perfectly in harmony with our overriding norm to attempt to provide for high levels of employment with incomes rising with productivity. The difference between such an undertaking and the undertaking to provide 'full employment' whatever happens is simply that, on the formula suggested, attempts to raise incomes above the increase of production at constant prices have no such guarantee. If the policy of organised groups involves a net increase of expenditure over the increase of aggregate production at constant prices, so that employment can only be maintained by inflation, then the promise of 'full employment' no longer holds. For the organisation concerned it is a matter of revising their claim or taking action which will reduce the volume of employment available. Put this way this recommendation may sound hard. But if it is realised that aggregate claims in excess of the norm inevitably involve inflation, it should not be unacceptable to any who do not wish to see the purchasing power of money indefinitely reduced.

But how should it be carried out? Here it must be candidly admitted that there is still much room for controversy.

For the present writer it seems clear that all policies of this sort must fail if regard is not had to the supply of money and credit. The bitter experience of the years in which it was the fashionable view that money could look after itself seems to be conclusive evidence of that. Further, I do not find myself in sympathy with the view of the Radcliffe Committee that the necessary control is best exercised by operation on the interest structure. There are so many rates of interest in the capital market, and such elusive relations between them, that in my judgement it is far better to operate directly on the money supply in the broad sense and to allow the consequential changes in interest rates to work themselves out spontaneously.

To this extent I would align myself with the views of Professor Friedman. I would also support his view that we know so little about the possibilities of short-term manipulation of money and credit that, as a first approximation, there is much to be said for a policy of attempting a more or less regular annual rise of the money supply adjustable to secular variations in productivity. As I understand it, this is not represented as a cure-all but rather as a lesser evil than less predictable manoeuvres.

Thus far I would go along with Professor Friedman's school of thought, and if to entertain the belief that control of the money supply is an essential feature of stabilisation policy is to be called a 'monetarist', then a monetarist I will be. I would not, however, pass a self-denying ordinance regarding all uses of the fiscal instrument. I would willingly agree that such instruments are very liable to abuse and have indeed been much abused in the past. The belief that our information regarding variations of national income is so precise that we can venture on fine-tuning of the economy by fiscal means with any confidence seems to me a reflection of the simplicity of those who entertain it, rather than an assurance of success. If fiscal policy is to be invoked at all I should much prefer some automatism, not necessarily identical with, but of the same kind foreshadowed by, Professor Meade's index-linked social-security contributions, rather than unpredictable antics by not particularly well-qualified, and not always well-advised, Chancellors. But a complete abdication of fiscal policy to meet any stabilisation contingencies is not a position with which I should wish to be identified. And in the progress, if it ever occurs, from a state bordering on hyperinflation to more normal conditions, I would say that fiscal policies have an important part to play.

In conclusion I would like to emphasise that control of aggregate expenditure is not a cure-all: it is merely a safeguard against inflation or deflation. Indeed it is not difficult to see how a policy of this sort may bring into the open structural deficiencies which otherwise may be veiled for a time by looseness in this area. Suppose there exists a tight monopoly in the supply of some goods or services in respect of which the elasticity of demand is low, that is to say where, despite price rises, consumers are willing to pay more to secure what they regard as essential supplies – some forms of energy for instance – and suppose that such a monopoly demands pay increases quite out of line with the rest. In that case with aggregate expenditure rising only with increases of productivity in general, demand for other things will be less, and consequently any unemployment which the excessive rise of incomes in the group concerned has caused will be thrown elsewhere: that is producers who have not made excessive claims will bear the burden.

It is in such instances that the demand for statutory control of pay seems most plausible. I have already shown that, at a time when positive general inflation is being brought under control, there is a possible case for temporary measures of this kind; and to the extent that monopoly practices of the sort supposed seem permanent, the case for control of this sort is reinforced. But in the long run this is a poor solution. It involves arbitrary judgement; it involves politics: it tends to spread. In the long run surely it is far better to choose the policy suggested in an earlier chapter, namely to make associations of producers of this sort subject to the general law relating to monopoly and restrictive practices. It is of course possible to conceive of conditions where technical factors and the resulting necessary absence of competition put supplies of it in the power of a handful of operatives to paralyse a whole community – exclusive power supply for a wide area from a single nuclear station for instance – in which case contracts of service involving sanctions as severe as military duty would be incumbent. But such conditions are likely to be rare. In normal circumstances, given a reasonable degree of stability in the value of money, much less stringent and more generally applicable regulations are necessary to prevent the emergencies of damaging monopolistic practices.

All that has been said so far on the stability of the system as a whole still abstracts from international complications. I shall return to these in a later chapter. For the time being I must proceed to consideration of other problems of a more general nature.

CHAPTER 7

Welfare and Distribution

POVERTY AND THE CLASSICAL TRADITION

Our survey, up to now, has been concerned principally with matters of machinery. The market mechanism works however the power to demand is distributed. It responds to demand from whatever quarter. The conditions of over-all stability – the avoidance of deflation or inflation in so far as our present knowledge makes this possible – may require different measures according to varying dispositions to save and invest; but, in general terms, they apply to societies at different stages of development and distribution of income. It is now time to turn to more concrete matters of wealth and poverty, distribution and social services. As before we shall take as our starting point the position of Classical Political Economy in these respects.

At the outset it is necessary to dispose of a widespread misapprehension. It is often supposed, quite genuinely by the lay public and, with less title to respect, by some persons who as professional economists should know better, that the Classical outlook was indifferent to the problems of poverty and that it has needed the exhortations of recent reformers to arouse any concern in this respect. The Classical Economists 'defended subsistence wages', as one well-known publicist declared in a work intended for popular consumption. And even where there is no such overt accusation, it is alleged that there was widespread indifference.

In fact few statements about the history of thought could be further from the truth; and their promulgation is a sure sign of historical illiteracy. It is quite true that in the earlier literature there are abundant examples of indifference to the fate of the poor or even vindication of the desirability of cheap labour.

Bernard Mandeville's chapter on 'Charity Schools' in the *Fable of the Bees* is a classical example of cynical nastiness in this respect; and the standard history of the subject, Furness's *Position of the Labourer in a System of Nationalism*, provides ample evidence of the widespread, if not universal, prevalence of this sort of thing in the centuries with which it deals. But to attribute such attitudes to the Classical Economists is pure travesty. Classical Political Economy was essentially concerned with what its exponents would have called 'improvement'; and this meant the general condition of the people. I have already quoted Adam Smith's definition of the object of political economy; 'to provide a plentiful revenue or subsistence for the people.'* Even more explicit is his famous statement that

> servants, labourers and workmen of different kinds make up the far greater part of every great political society. But what improves the circumstances of the greater part can never be regarded as an inconvenience to the whole. No society can be flourishing and happy of which the far greater part of the members are poor and miserable. It is but equity, besides, that they who feed cloathe and lodge the whole body of the people, should have such a share of their own labour as to be themselves tolerably well fed cloathed and lodged.†

I have written at length elsewhere quoting similar sentiments from representative Classical Economists from Malthus, Ricardo, James Mill, McCulloch and Senior; and it would be otiose to repeat the process.‡ That the Classical Economists were concerned with growth, and that their concern was especially orientated on the possible effects of growth in redeeming the conditions of the majority of the people stands out in any just appraisal. It is difficult not to believe that those who deny it, do so because, consciously or unconsciously, they do not want to recognise it: a platform for high-minded denunciation of persons intellectually and morally considerably more admirable than they themselves would vanish beneath their feet if they were to do so. But to clinch matters it may be

*See above p. 1.
†*Wealth of Nations*, vol.i, p. 80.
‡See my *Theory of Economic Policy in English Classical Political Economy*, ch. iii.

worth citing John Stuart Mill whose avowed purpose it was to synthesise the system and relate it to social philosophy. 'Whether the aggregate produce increases absolutely or not', he writes in the famous chapter on the 'Probable Futurity of the Labouring Classes', 'is not a thing in which after a certain amount has been obtained, neither the legislature nor the philanthropist need feel any strong interest; but that it should *increase relatively to the number of those who share in it, is of the utmost possible importance*' [my italics].*

If we come to more recent history, any contention that the great followers of this tradition, Sidgwick, Marshall, Pigou, Robertson – and here Keynes would not wish to be excluded – were not interested, according to their lights, in the redemption of poverty must be regarded as either deliberate misrepresentation or a lack of perceptiveness calling imperatively for very sympathetic psychiatric treatment.

GROWTH AND POVERTY

It was a basic approach of the Classical tradition that the general raising of standards of living must come from increases in production per head. As we shall see, this did not exclude the raising of some standards by transfers; nor did it exclude the possibility of raising productivity by such means. But then, as now, the quantitative perspective was clear: the extent to which income per head could be raised by redistribution had limits far below what was conceivable in terms of increases in average production; and there can be no doubt that the main, but by no means the only, hope of the Classical writers lay in this direction.

This leaps to the mind at once if we reflect upon their general approbation of the results of a system of division of labour guided by market forces. It was not because this enriched European princes 'but because it brought it about that "the accommodation of industrial and frugal peasants" exceeded that of many an African King' that it evoked Adam Smith's memorable eulogy.† But this comes out even more clearly if we recall the specific treatment of certain matters relating to

Principles of Political Economy, p. 758.
†*Wealth of Nations*, vol. I, p. 9.

growth and wages. We may consider these under the three heads of invention, accumulation and population control.

Invention

There can be no doubt of the considerable hopes based on the growth of knowledge relevant to productivity per head. One of the main advantages of the division of labour highlighted in Adam Smith's famous exposition in the *Wealth of Nations* was 'the invention of a great number of machines which facilitate and abridge labour, and enable one man to do the work of many'. And belief in the power of invention to benefit the condition of humanity in general, and the working classes in particular, runs through the main tradition of the Classical thought. The propagandist works of Knight, William Ellis and, on a different plane, Harriet Martineau's stories, are direct reflections of the propositions and convictions of the main figures of the school.*

The apparent exception is Ricardo. As is well known, he changed his mind on this subject and with characteristic candour admitted as much. In the famous chapter on machinery in the Third Edition of his *Principles*,† he relates that 'ever since he turned his attention to questions to political economy' he had been of the opinion that 'such an application of machinary to any branch of production, as should have the effect of saving labour, was a general good accompanied only with that portion of inconvenience which in most cases attends the removal of capital and labour from one employment to another'. He thought that landlords and capitalists would benefit and that 'the class of labourers also "would be" equally benefited by the use of machinery as they would have the means of buying more commodities with the same money wages'; and he thought 'that no reduction of wages would take place because the capitalist would have the power of demanding and employing the same quantity of labour as before'. But now he had come to the view that this was erroneous and that 'the opinion entertained by the labouring class that the employment of

*Charles Knight, *The Results of Machinery* (1830), William Ellis, *Outline of Social Economy* (1860), Harriet Martineau, *Illustration, of Political Economy* (1856) 9 vols.
†*Works*, ed. Sraffa, vol. i, pp. 386–97.

machinery is frequently detrimental to their interest is not founded on prejudice and error but is conformable to the correct principles of political economy'.

This perception that the introduction of machinery may conceivably involve shifts in the demand for labour which actually lower the equilibrium wage level occasioned great consternation in the breast of McCulloch, at that time one of Ricardo's most devoted admirers. 'If your reasoning . . . be well founded', he wrote, 'the laws against the Luddites are a disgrace to the statute book'.* In fact, as we now know, the circumstances in which Ricardo's analysis would be relevant are not likely to be frequent. As Mill argued later† and as Sir John Hicks has demonstrated recently,‡ they are most likely to occur in primitive conditions when machinery is introduced for the first time. But, in any case, the concession to the arguments against the traditional position on the beneficial effects of inventions was more apparent than real. For, as Ricardo himself went on to argue, even if the adverse effect were to take place, it was essentially for a short period, since the savings that would accrue from the growing class of landowners and capitalists would itself augment the demand for labour. Such savings, he said, being annual, 'must soon create a fund much greater than the loss of the gross revenue, originally lost by the discovery of the machine, when the demand for labour will be as great as before, and the situation of the people will be still further improved by the increased savings which the increased net revenue will enable them to make.'§

It can therefore be confidently asserted that, whatever the possibilities disclosed for a pure theory of distributive shares, Ricardo's change of view on machinery and the demand for labour cannot be held to have made serious inroads in the Classical belief in the beneficial effects of inventions on the

Works, ed. Sraffa, vol. VIII, pp. 384–5.
†*Principles of Political Economy* (Toronto edition) p. 97.
‡J. R. Hicks, *Capital and Time* (Oxford University Press, 1973) pp. 97–9. There is an interesting discussion of Ricardo's proposition in Wicksell's *Lectures on Political Economy* (1934) vol. I, pp. 133–44. For McCulloch's animadversions on the subject through discussions in successive editions of his *Principles* see Professor O'Brien's masterly work, *J. R. McCulloch: A Study in Classical Economics* (London: Allen & Unwin, 1970)
§*Works*, ed. Sraffa, vol. I, p. 396.

growth of production per head and its consequent implications for the potential diminution of poverty. In recent years, of course, this confidence has been fortified both by experience and by theoretical developments not directly contemplated by the Classical authority. Having regard to the rise of real wages of the industrial countries it would be difficult to argue that the aggregate effect of invention has been adverse to the interest of labour. And, since the maintenance of the incentive to invest is now held to be one of the main safeguards against any deflationary tendencies of the disposition to save, there is additional reason for believing common sense in this connection.

Accumulation

As regards accumulation, while, as we have seen, there were those such as Malthus and his followers who argued that it could be excessive, for the main Classical tradition belief in its benefits was fundamental. Accumulation, from the Classical point of view, provided, *inter alia*, what Adam Smith called 'the funds destined for the maintenance of labour' – to all intents and purposes what John Stuart Mill called the Wage Fund. We need not discuss here to what extent, under static conditions, this fund was regarded as flexible. The significant point here is the emphasis that the greater the volume of these funds in relation to the size of the working population, the greater the competition among the employers and the higher therefore the level of wages. To a very considerable extent this was the rationale of the strong commendation of saving which was forthcoming from the majority of the members of this school. Thus the increase of accumulation was one of the main ingredients in their hope for the improvement of the lot of the common man.

Population Control

The final ingredient, of course, was population control – the hope that realisation of the connection between numbers and income per head would eventually influence the rate of increase. If the general level of wages depended on the one side on 'the funds destined for the maintenance of labour' and on the other side on the size of the labour force, then, if numbers were controlled, increasing accumulation would cause wages to rise. It was this belief which inspired Ricardo's famous hope that 'in all countries the labouring classes should have a taste for comforts and enjoyments and that they should be stimulated by all legal means in their exertions to procure them'.* It was this belief which made Bentham and his followers, conspicuously Francis Place, pioneers of the birth-control movement in this country and inspired James Mill's claim that due limitation of numbers could raise the condition of the labourer to 'any state of comfort and enjoyment which may be desired'.†

I need hardly say that, from the modern point of view, we should regard this claim as somewhat exaggerated. We recognise much more clearly than did the Classical writers the possibility of *under-* as well as *over-population*, that is conditions in which an increase of numbers of active workers would be accompanied by increasing returns per head. It is also easy to conceive conditions in which, in some state of technical knowledge and accumulated wealth, the level of income per head with an optimal population might not necessarily be all that might be desired. Moreover it must be admitted that the whole idea of optimality in regard to population is very much in the air: there are no ways known to me of giving precision to the concept.‡

Nevertheless we should certainly agree that over-population in this sense is not only conceivable but has existed at various times and places and probably exists today. I personally believe that, even in the countries of the Western World, the wage and salary earning classes would have much to gain, even from the narrowly economic point of view – to say nothing of wider considerations of amenity – from limiting their numbers to a more or less stationary condition. And I am quite sure that if such limitation does not occur in many of the so-called underdeveloped countries, we shall soon be faced with demographic catastrophes without precedent in history.

*Ibid. vol. 1, p. 100.
†Mill, *Elements of Political Economy*, 3rd edn (1844) p.67.
‡For a brief discussion of some of the difficulties see my *Theory of Economic Development*, pp. 41–3.

THE CLASSICAL TRADITION AND INEQUALITY

There can be no doubt that the central Classical tradition rested its main hope of improvement – the general raising of living standards – on the growth of productive power. And equally there can be no doubt that in the light of history it was right. Much as has been done by way of the relief of poverty and the spread of certain services by transfers between classes, it is not open to serious question that the main influence in raising the lot of the poorer classes of society has been due to increases in production per head due to the positive influences already discussed: invention and accumulation outweighing any adverse effects of undue population increase.

This does not mean, however, that the tradition was indifferent to matters of distribution. It is sometimes said that it was not interested in equalising tendencies. This is not correct. It is true that, given the framework of law and order – which incidentally involved a strong belief in equality before the law – it believed in private property and the market as organising agents; and although, as we shall see, there are important equalising tendencies in the operation of free markets, there is no reason to suppose that the end-product of such agency, as regards the distribution of income or property, will be a state of equality. That is why, believing in the superior efficiency of this institution of economic freedom, it was sceptical of systems which promised continuing equality all round – there will be more to say about this later on when I discuss the political economy of Total Collectivism. It is also true that, confronted with policies which diminished production per head but which involved more equal distribution of the remainder, its attitude would probably have been negative, on the ground that, in the end, the absolute relief of poverty *per se* was more important than the diminution of inequality. But it is not true that, other things being equal, it was indifferent to problems of distribution or hostile to equalising tendencies. It must be remembered that the members of this school were, in the broad sense, utilitarians; and it is incontestable that, again other things being equal, this point of view favoured less inequality. 'The establishment of equality', said Bentham, 'is a chimera; the only thing which can be done is to diminish inequality.'* I think the same can be said of those who at the present day still cherish the ideal of Liberalism.

But why should this be so? What are the legitimate reasons for favouring measures which diminish inequality of income or wealth?

They certainly cannot be said to rest on solid belief in a prospect of extensive increases in income per head from general levelling processes. Misinformed generosity is apt to assume immense potentialities in such measures. But this is not so. All serious statistical investigation has shown that, even assuming no diminution of incentive and production, even in the richer countries, completely egalitarian redistribution would involve a comparatively insignificant rise in income per head. From this point of view, inequality creates an illusion, somewhat similar to that which might arise from unreflecting contemplation of the effect of the levelling of mountains: the net effect in most cases would be the raising of the average height above sea level by a few inches. In spite of the many redistributive measures of this century, few things can be more certain than that the main rise in the Western World of the incomes of the poorer classes has been due to increases in productivity.

We may dismiss further belief in the intrinsic merits of enforced economic equality all round. Equality of opportunity – *la carrière ouverte aux talents* – is indeed a desirable objective; and the fostering of such a state of affairs by the abolition of discrimination and the provision of facilities for investment in education have always been Liberal preoccupations. But equality of the *results* of such equality – that surely is quite another matter. It is one thing to say that, short of the abolition of the family, every effort will be made to secure equal facilities for training for, and equal access to, various occupations: it is quite another to say that, whatever use is made of such opportunities, the rewards of effort will be equal. It may well be that in certain walks of life the discharge of ghostly offices, as the eighteenth century called them, for instance the maxim of equal pay for unequal dedication, is perhaps sensible, although it cannot always be said to have been practised – to put it

* *Works*, ed. John Bowring (1843) vol. I, p. 311.

mildly. But over the greater part of the field it is a recipe for inefficiency and makes nonsense of the whole basis of the principle of equal opportunity. Equal opportunity to win equal prizes – a dodo race for the world.

It is arguable, and I happen to believe it, that once he has obtained a reasonable competence for his family and himself, a sensible man with a job which interests him should not worry over much about what superior awards are available for others. The fact that some prize boxers and popular singers can earn perhaps fifty times as much as most academics is not worth the loss of five minutes sleep on the part of the latter class – though it sometimes seems as if it does. But an inhibition on aspiring to superior income from greater effort, should the impulse, or the belief of need, exist, is not something which a free society should impose or indeed cultivate. A healthy society cannot flourish on a basis of green-eye; and the fact that there is so much green-eye implicit or explicit in the politics of contemporary society is one of the reasons for sometimes doubting its eventual survival, save as totalitarian tyranny.

There are, however, more legitimate reasons for favouring policies which involve greater equality. Stated broadly they are three.

First there is the principle of burden sharing. The expenses of the state necessarily involve some appropriation of individual income; and although the purposes of taxation are inevitably complex and involve more than one objective, it is usually accepted that justice involves some degree of progression in the burden thus imposed. This does not depend on the somewhat specious precision of the Benthamite 'felicific calculus', itself avowedly founded on convention; surely more time and ingenuity has been wasted upon alternative completely un-proveable hypotheses about the rate at which the so-called social marginal utility of income diminishes in this connection than upon most other speculation in Political Economy. The solid basis for some progression in taxation is the common-sense presumption that the loss of a pound is more significant to most poor men than to most rich men.

The second presumption in favour of equalising tendencies is the desirability of more centres of independent initiative. There are few guarantees of personal freedom more effective than a reserve of capital wealth; and both politics and economic activity stand to benefit from a wide diffusion of such positions. Those who believe in the beneficial potentialities of private property in some form or other should believe, too, in the maxim of Francis Bacon that 'money is like muck not good except it be spread'.*

The third ground favouring measures involving greater equality is the positive desirability of assistance to various forms of poverty and distress and some supplements to family provision for meeting certain needs. These are matters involving many different issues in different connections which will be the subject of more extensive discussion at a later stage of the argument. At the present juncture it is necessary only to note that the levelling-up process involved here is, so to speak, an obverse aspect of the case for differential burden sharing which was the first of our arguments for equalising tendencies.

The remainder of this chapter will be devoted, first to discussing the role of markets in this connection and, secondly, the influences of income and capital taxation. The problems of various forms of assistance and relief will be the subject of the following chapter.

PRICE AND INCOME FIXING

Let me begin by stating baldly that mitigation of inequality by direct interference with competitive markets is no part of the programme of Liberal Political Economy, ancient or modern. To depress prices below the equilibrium point is to invite shortages. To fix rates of pay above the point which clears the market is to manufacture unemployment or inflation.

In each case there are, of course, exceptions. In siege conditions Liberal economists may well recommend price-fixing when it is accompanied by rationing and authoritarian control of supply. And over the wide field of the so-called public utility and the nationalised undertakings, it is clear that some form of supervision of price policy – the more flexible the better – is dictated by the nature of the enterprise. But where goods and services are provided under reasonably competitive

---

Bacon's Essays, ed. Thomas Whately (1855), 'On Seditions and Troubles', p. 144.

conditions all experience shows that price-fixing which is not merely nominal, i.e. that which simply follows the market, runs into difficulties. Unless the elasticity of demand is zero it at once creates excess demand and a tendency to a falling off of supply. The extent to which this latter tendency manifests itself immediately depends upon the nature of the commodity. Stocks of perishables tend not to be replenished almost at once; durables of which the existing stock greatly exceeds the annual production take longer to be affected. During the wars of this century when price-fixing prevailed, special controls had to be imposed almost at once to maintain essential supplies of food. The fixing of rents did not at first greatly affect the supply of accommodation; but fifty years of 'housing shortage' and maldistribution in all countries practising rent control attest the eventual effects of policies of this sort.

The purpose of price control of this sort is obviously to save the pockets of the poorer members of the community – an objective to which, in itself, no exception can be taken, indeed quite the contrary. But the method is misconceived. To fix the price of, say, meat below the level which clears the market not only involves complications on the demand side, it also involves subsidies of some sort, if supply is not to be inadequate. It follows therefore that all sorts of people who could afford higher prices benefit equally with those who cannot. It is an entirely wasteful use of public money. The same result, the relief of the needy, could be obtained at far less cost by cash allowances to those whose incomes fall below a certain level. Whether this is good policy or bad is a matter which will need further investigation. But it should be clear that there are cheaper ways of helping the poor than by subsidising the well-to-do.

As for rates of pay, the general presumptions are similar. It is possible to conceive of labour markets, in which poor and ignorant labourers are confronted by ruthless combinations of employers, where intervention to prevent exploitation may well be justified. But indiscriminate minimum wage-fixing certainly runs the danger of doing more harm than good. Even if, for the average worker in the area concerned, it does nothing but confirm average rates which would have been established by market forces, it may easily exclude from employment the less able and the positively subnormal. There seems little doubt that intervention of this sort has prejudiced the employment of coloured labour in various parts of the world; and it is easy to conceive of instances where it may facilitate discrimination against women. There are certainly better ways of helping those who are below the average in skill and strength than by making it unprofitable to employ them.

THE MARKET AS EQUALISER

To reject direct interference with competitive markets, how-ever, is not to reject policies having equalising tendencies; and in this connection it deserves emphasis that, part at least, of the Classical emphasis on the benefits of competition rested in fact on just this influence. Where competition is possible, there exceptional gains are likely to be transitory: mobility of labour and capital tends positively to eliminate inequalities. The Classical Economists, especially of the earlier period, were confronted by a state of affairs in which all sorts of monopolistic positions were supported by law or administrative custom; and much of their arguments were directed to eliminating them. It was not only in the interests of productive efficiency that they opposed such abuses, it was also because they gave rise to positions of what from their point of view was unjustified privilege.

It is the same outlook which has inspired the anti-monopoly and anti-restrictive-practices legislation of more recent years. It is not only because monopoly may result in an allocation of resources less favourable to optimal production that such measures are supported: it is also because such positions and practices give rise to opportunities denied to those able and willing to exploit them and so lead to inequalities which other-wise would not exist. We all know the case against giant corporations misusing monopoly power; it is sometimes the cliché of the tub-thumper, sometimes abundantly justified. It is less frequently mentioned that the practices of the closed shop or requirements of unnecessary qualifications for profes-sional work of one kind and another, which limit would-be applicants to those parts of the labour market where they prevail, are open to similar objections. It is incontestable that they have been – and still are – productive of much inequality and injustice. In appraising the bias – if that be the appropriate word – of the Classical writers and their successors in favour of competitive markets, the equalising aspect of this operation should certainly not be overlooked.

TAXATION AND INEQUALITY

The Classical tradition, however, was not content to leave the diminution of inequality to the free play of competitive forces. It discussed further, and advocated, policies directed to this end, either through the tax system or through positive measures directed to the equalisation of opportunity. The first of these groups, tax instruments, will be the remaining subject of this chapter, the second will be part of more general discussion of welfare and relief.

Taxation of Income

We may begin our survey with policies relating to the taxation of income.

So far as this problem is concerned, the interesting issue is between proportionality and progressiveness in taxation. Proportionality, while placing the heavier absolute burden on the larger incomes, leaves inequality unchanged, progressiveness changes it according to the degree adopted.

On this issue the tradition is ambiguous. Adam Smith's canon that taxation should be in proportion to ability to pay* can be used to justify either principle, according to whether proportionality be conceived in relation to money or in relation to the convention that marginal utility of income diminishes as incomes become larger – a principle which can probably be sustained on introspective grounds, so far as individuals are concerned, but which goes far beyond introspection or observation in that it implies a comparison of capacity for satisfaction between individuals; and one can discover passages in Adam Smith's *Wealth of Nations* which could be used to justify either interpretation. The canon itself seems to imply proportionality in money terms. But elsewhere, in the discussion of house rents,

Wealth of Nations, vol. II, p. 350.

Smith permits himself to say explicitly that 'it is not unreasonable that the rich should contribute to the public expense, not only in proportion, but something more than in that proportion'.*

In sharp contrast to this we find John Stuart Mill arguing strongly against progression, although his attitude to inequality of capital was, as we shall see, very radical indeed. He was in favour of an exemption of a minimum subsistence level – which mathematically involves a degree of progressiveness in the rest. But beyond this he contended that

> to tax the larger incomes at a higher percentage than the small is to lay a tax on industry and economy, to impose a penalty on people for having worked harder and saved more than their neighbours. A just and wise legislature would abstain from holding out motives for dissipating rather than saving the earnings of honest exertion. Its impartiality between competitors would consist in endeavouring to see that all should start fair, and *not in hanging a weight on the swift to diminish the distance between them and the slow* [my italics].†

I must confess that I find a good deal more cogency in Mill's argument than do probably many of my contemporaries. Clearly, by itself, it could be used to justify either a proportionate income tax or a tax on general expenditure – though because of his recommendation of an exemption limit for the former, and different rates as between earned and unearned income, I doubt if Mill would have been prepared to use it that way. But, combined with his other 'heretical' opinion that an ordinary income tax taxes savings twice, which has much authority behind it, it does furnish support for considerable reliance on sales taxes and the like, and up to a point I personally would favour these also on the ground that they are likely to be less damaging to incentive than corresponding rates of direct taxation. The arguments against this view are well known: it implies irrationality and inability to distinguish real income from money income. But it is still probably true to much motivation as we observe it.

---

*Ibid. vol. ɪɪ, p. 368. See also the approval of higher tolls on luxury vehicles (vol. ɪɪ, p. 246).
†*Principles of Political Economy*, pp. 810–11.

Having said this, however, I must add at once that I am not (repeat *not*) opposed to some degree of progressiveness in direct taxation – not on the grounds of pseudo-exact interpersonal comparisons of utility, but simply on Adam Smith's common-sense observations, already cited, that 'it is not unreasonable that the rich should contribute not only in proportion but something more than in that proprtion'. But I hasten to say that I think that this can very easily be overdone. We have heard a great deal about the lack of evidence concerning the disincentive effect of income taxation; and I agree that there may well be an area of uncertainty here. We also hear a lot about the best work being done for non-pecuniary motives – and I admit that creative artists, great social reformers and many admirable humbler people are not governed chiefly by the cash incentive. It is hard to believe that anyone but a complete imbecile ever thought the contrary: economists make life too easy for themselves if they claim deep insight for what is common knowledge. But in the ordinary work of the world the pecuniary incentive does play an important role; and if we keep clearly in mind – what all sorts of people (who should know better) conveniently forget – that it is the *marginal* rather than the *average* rate which is more relevant, it is really very implausible indeed to contend that high rates may not deter. I suppose that all but the completely unworldly would agree that a marginal rate of 100 per cent would have some adverse effects on the disposition to work or save of most ordinary people. Why then assume that the rates which actually prevail in the United Kingdom in the present day should not operate the same way? Is it really to be supposed that the disincentive is absent until one reaches 99·9 per cent and then suddenly becomes complete?

My conclusion, then, in this connection is that a moderate degree of progression in direct taxation may well be used at once to raise revenue and to diminish inequality, but that, if pushed far, it may well have adverse consequences. In my opinion a diminution of inequality brought about in this way, which at the same time involved any substantial brake on the increase of production, in the present circumstances of most communities would be a very poor exchange. This, I need hardly say, is a value judgement.

Taxation of Capital

When we come to the distribution of capital wealth the possibilities are different.

I take it that there is no need to argue the case against periodic redistribution on an egalitarian basis, whether every seven years, as suggested in the Pentateuch, or at other intervals. The confusion would be intolerable and the effect on the disposition to accumulate highly adverse. But this does not begin to exhaust the subject.

We may start from Bentham's dictum that it is 'at the moment of death' that operations affecting distribution are most convenient and have least effect on the incentive to accumulate.* At this point two alternative principles are conceivable; operation on the estate as a whole or operations on the sections into which it is divided – in U.K. practice these in the past were described as 'estate duties' or 'legacy duties' respectively.

Now there can be no doubt that progressive estate duties can affect distribution. In spite of widespread evasion by gifts *inter vivos* – which of course increases as the rates become more penal – they do take large sums from higher fortunes; and to that extent they diminish inequality. But, if as is practised at present, the proceeds are used for current expenditure, they may easily tend to diminish accumulation more than other ways of raising revenue.

Much to be preferred in my judgement is the legacy-duty principle. Here the progression *is on the sum received rather than on the fortune out of which it is paid*. There is therefore a clear incentive to testators to diminish the total subtraction from the estate by spreading the bequests. Although, at given rates, the sum taken by the state will be less, the distribution of wealth will be broadened: and, from the point of view of a Liberal political economist, this is, in itself, a desirable objective. I should perhaps add that there is nothing administratively impracticable about this principle; for years duties on legacies were part of the U.K. system. But they were overshadowed by the estate duty and eventually, partly I suspect on grounds of Socialist theory, partly for reasons of administrative simplification, they were abolished – in my judgement, the wrong abolition.

*Bentham, *Works*, vol. 1, p. 312.

E

It is worth noting that John Stuart Mill made a much more radical suggestion. He proposed that there should be set an upper limit which any single person should receive by gifts or inheritance. I personally would not wish to go as far as this. It would clearly involve great administrative complications and be a standing invitation to fraudulent evasion. For similar reasons I do not favour taxation on gifts between the living although I recognise some inverted logic in extending in this way the principle of this kind of death duty. I am also against it on the more general ground that the absence of such taxation is some incentive to transfers from the old to the young, which is a state I prefer to that exemplified by Shakespeare's 'dowager Long lingering out a young man's revenue'. But on all such questions I am far from obstinate conviction. The point on which I would insist is the desirability of using the tax incentive to *spread* property ownership rather than to *destroy* it.

CHAPTER 8

Welfare and Distribution (continued)

DISTRIBUTION AND PUBLIC EXPENDITURE: PRINCIPLES

So far in my discussion of welfare and distribution my main preoccupations have been with the growth of production per head as the main hope of diminution of poverty and with the mitigation of inequality by the instrumentality of competition and the tax system. But this is not the end of the subject. It should be clear that the uses to which the proceeds of taxation are put must play an important role in the determination of the general welfare. These include the increase of equality of opportunity, the relief of need and the provision of indiscriminate benefit. The main principles involved will be the subject of this chapter.

In discussing the problems which arise we shall find ourselves confronted with conflicts of aim and conflicts of method – for example the desirability of alleviating family indigence and the undesirability of promoting an indiscriminate increase of population. Most of these are better dealt with in connection with specific problems. But there is one overriding principle springing from the fundamentals of Classical Liberalism, which deserves discussion at the outset, namely the desirability, within practical limits, of enlarging freedom of choice and limiting paternalism, even in regard to problems of assistance and relief.

The issues at stake here are nowhere better stated than in the opening sections of John Stuart Mill's famous chapter on 'The Probable Future of the Labouring Classes'* in his contrast between what he calls the theory of dependence and protection

Principles of Political Economy, pp. 758–62.

and the theory of self-dependence. Mill is there discussing the attitude of paternalism in general – 'It is supposed to be the duty of the higher classes to think for "the poor", and to take the responsibility for their lot as the commander and officers of an army take that of the soldiers composing it.' But his animadversions have a wider significance than in this context. If the aim of Classical Liberalism in the wide sense be the general raising of the condition of the people, the objective governing the relief of the indigent should be, as far as possible, to foster independence and to create for them the same sense of initiative and responsibility as middle-class reformers automatically assume for themselves, as for instance in the choice of food, housing, medical attention, provision for family education, and so on. Clearly it would be folly to apply this principle in full rigour to primitive peoples or persons in a state of acute mental and physical degradation – and there are still many instances of such categories. But in the civilisation of the West, where now, for the most part, average incomes approach what would have been described as artisan or lower middle class even fifty years ago, there seems no sufficient reason for any more paternalism for them as for those whom the Victorians would have called 'their superiors', although as we shall see, for reasons quite extraneous to this argument, the drift of policy has been mainly the other way.

Thus, if this position be accepted, where measures for the mitigation of poverty or distress are concerned, there is a presumption in favour of relief in *cash* rather than in *kind* and *free cash* rather than cash *tied to particular* forms of expenditure. Even where the balance of argument is in favour of greater specificity, as in the cases we shall shortly be discussing, there is still a prescription in favour of as much freedom of choice as the circumstances permit.

EDUCATION – BASIC

We may begin our reflections on this part of our subject by some survey of the main issues in regard to what may be called 'basic education', that is the education of all children capable of being educated up to a certain school-leaving age.

It should be well known, though apparently it often is not,

that the Classical Economists were among the pioneers in advocating state intervention to ensure a minimum education throughout the community at large. This rested partly on grounds of production efficiency and capacity to perform the duties of citizenship. Adam Smith, whose exposition of the advantages of the division of labour is famous, explained also that, unless offset by some degree of general education, it might have the disadvantage of depriving the mass of the people of intellectual breadth and martial virtues. He thought it was a proper function of the state to provide this offset. Partly, however, the position rested upon a more fundamental recognition of the rights of children. As Senior, often regarded as an ogre of reaction by the manufacturers of fictitious social history, forcefully put it, in his *Suggestions on Popular Education*, 'it is as much the duty of the community to see that the child is educated as to see that it is fed' and 'unless the community can and will compel the parent to feed the child, the community must do so'.*

The legitimacy of imposing compulsion on parents to produce evidence that their children are being educated is not a matter which, it is to be hoped, would need any argument nowadays, though in the days of the Classical Economists it was still a controversial matter. Nor should it be disputed that, where the means to do so do not exist, then, in some way or other, they should be provided. This, too, was a doctrine propounded by the Classical Economists.

But this does not settle the question of *how* provision should be made. As things have actually developed in the United Kingdom, this has been answered by the provision of state schools *plus* some degree of subsidy for special denominational institutions, first in the sphere of primary education, then later, where secondary education is concerned, the state has provided schools where the services involved are provided free or with highly subsidised fees. Thus the obligation on parents to ensure that their children receive education has been joined by the provision *in kind* of the services necessary for those who care to take them.

But clearly this is not the only way in which the provision

*See my *Theory of Economic Development*, pp. 75–82 for quotations and a fuller treatment of this subject.

could be met: and, if the views of John Stuart Mill had been regarded, a different method might have been adopted. 'If the Government would make up its mind to *require* for every child a good education', he said in his essay *On Liberty*, 'it might save itself the trouble of *providing* one. It might leave to parents to obtain the education where and how they pleased and content itself with helping to pay the school fees of the poorer classes of children and defraying the entire school expenses of those who have no one else to pay for them'; and he goes on to argue that

> a general state education is a mere contrivance for moulding people to be exactly like one another; and as the mould in which it casts them is that which pleases the predominant power in the government . . . in proportion as it is efficient it establishes a despotism over the mind, leading by natural tendency to one over the body. An education established and controlled by the state should only exist, if it exists at all, as one among many competing experiments, carried on for the purpose of example and stimulus to keep the others up to a certain standard of excellence.*

Such an alternative, although, having regard to what has happened since, clearly not within the bounds of probability today, is not intrinsically impracticable. Doubtless it might have to be accompanied by some suspension of the rule of *caveat emptor*, in the shape of periodic inspection to eliminate the possibility of the occasional emergence of *Do-the-boys Halls*. But it would certainly harmonise with the freedom of parental choice which is still postulated for well-to-do parents.

I say 'is still postulated'. But perhaps this needs qualification. For in our own day there has arisen a strong school of thought which, inspired by the fanaticism of equality, would abolish all independent opportunities of school education and force all children to attend the same type of school in localities pre-scribed, not by parental choice but rather by the elected majorities of the local-government authorities responsible.

There can be no doubt whatever that this is the very opposite of Liberalism whatever intelligible – as distinct from political – interpretation can be put on that word; and I think it doubly unfortunate that it has become associated with the idea of the

On Liberty (1859) pp. 190-1.

Comprehensive School which has attracted so much idealism and so much splendid educational talent in our day. Given the system of state provision which, as I have said already, must be taken as a *fait accompli* for this, and many future, days, I personally welcome the idea of schools which, like the so-called 'public schools',* are open to receive various types of children. The process of sorting out talent at the tender age of eleven or twelve, which prevailed when the separation of secondary modern and secondary grammar schools was the usual rule, seems to me educationally ridiculous and socially hateful; and I hope that the contemporary developments will be as successful as some of them already seem to be. But the idea of reducing all the variety of school provision to one pattern on which all children must be educated seems to realise all Mill's worst fears and, at the same time, although this would be denied by its advocates, to come perilously near what we have seen in our own day in the school education of the totalitarian countries. It only needs one further step in the same egalitarian direction to attain the odious system recommended in Plato's *Republic* of taking over infants at birth to remove all possible causes of inequality due to unequal parental influences.

It is to be hoped therefore that the many men and women of goodwill who have been ensnared by these tendencies will look once again at Mill, whose integrity and idealism very few would call in question, and ask whether such contemporary nostrums are really in the interests of progress to the good society.

FURTHER EDUCATION

The provision from public funds of a minimum of education does not exhaust the problem of providing equality of opportunity, or, better said – since complete equality could only be achieved by the abolition of the family – of minimising inequality. Many forms of leadership and skill demand education extending beyond this point; and both experience and statistical analysis show that a substantial proportion of the relevant age groups possess the capacity to benefit by it. But not all who

*For American readers it should be explained that in this context 'public' means 'private',

possess this capacity possess the means to finance its development – indeed it is almost certain that a substantial fraction do not. Their opportunities are therefore inferior to those of the minority who have sufficient means at their disposal. If, therefore, the policy of *la carrière ouverte aux talents* is to be pursued, it follows that adequate advances should be made from public sources to finance study in the various forms of higher and further education. I may say *en passant* that this is often to be recommended on grounds, not merely of distributive justice but also of productive efficiency. Such education is probably to be regarded as a good in itself for those who can benefit by it; and certainly it would be wrong to argue that there is any very obvious correlation between the extent of such training and the rate of economic growth. But it remains true that, broadly speaking, it is unwise to neglect the cultivation of potential productivity which higher and further education makes possible.

To return, however, to considerations of distribution, it is clearly in the interests of the equalising of opportunity that capacity should have access to advances. But it is equally in the interests of distributive justice that, if these advances result in superior incomes, they should be repaid. If this does not happen, then in so far as the funds from which they are made are raised by general taxation, it may justly be said that this taxation may tend to *create* inequality – to finance superior talent at the expense, partially at any rate, of talent which is not superior – a subsidy to the clever from the unclever.

This analysis has always seemed to me to be quite irrefutable. The reasons why it has not been made a general basis for policy are chiefly that to finance higher education by simple loans has itself grave disadvantages. Investment in human capital – and clearly that is a legitimate way of conceiving such finance – is a risky business. The promise may not be realised; or the eventual choice of occupation or way of life may not be such as to bring the pecuniary advantages which make repayment possible. Parents and possible candidates, therefore, may well be deterred from assuming this responsibility – a consideration which is the more likely to be operative the lower the family income. And where young women are concerned, the prospect of having to bring to the altar what may be regarded as a *negative* dowry may well be a severe deterrent, although, from the social point of view, it is surely important that future mothers with high intelligence potential should be educated as well as future fathers of like category. But, as Professor Prest has suggested,* such difficulties would not arise if the advances took the form, not of *unconditionally* repayable loans, but rather of loans which were *only repayable* when the financial position of the borrower had reached a certain level at which repayment was not an intolerable burden; and the business of collection would be a simple extension of the business of the Inland Revenue. It is true enough that the achievement of such an income may not in fact be due to the higher education actually taken. But it would be commonly regarded as fair evidence of capacity to repay the original privilege of superior opportunity. Arguments of this sort are not particularly popular in the United Kingdom where non-repayable maintenance and grants for fees have recently been the order of the day. But as the financial burden of more widespread education increases I have little doubt that their urgency will be generally realised.

The problem remains, however, what principle of eligibility for assistance of this sort should be adopted.

It is sometimes thought that such provision can be made on the basis of the policy which is called manpower planning. Detailed estimates should be made of the 'need' for the various qualifications and skills required in the period under consideration; and these will determine the intake and structure of further education in the community concerned. The plan will govern the number of admissions to various institutions and departments and the courses of study provided. Something of this sort is attempted in Soviet Russia: and in free societies much thought has been devoted to the technique and structure of such estimates, which clearly have a strong appeal to simple-minded believers in an 'orderly' society.

Now, of course, it is not to be denied that where government policy dictates certain requirements and establishments – the number of schools and size of classes for instance – it is possible to calculate the numbers of teachers needed; and it is sensible that this should be done. Indeed, unless one has regard to the vicissitudes of government policies in such respects, it is odd

*A. R. Prest, *Financing University Education* (Institute of Economic Affairs, 1966).

that so little of this has been done in the past. But the belief that such computations are typical of what is possible or compatible with the principles of a free society is based on illusion, an illusion which it is desirable to dissipate.

Thus it is erroneous to suppose that, outside certain categories, such as teaching and military service, which can be determined by policy, internal and external, the 'need' for technical services of a specialised kind is capable of easy prediction. Leaving aside consumers' demand, itself the subject of many unexpected vicissitudes, techniques change and with such changes the 'need' for different categories of service. Even the Russians admit that developments in electroincs upset the anticipations of manpower planning. Moreover, even if technique remained constant, the combinations of various kinds of manpower and equipment which it is sensible to adopt must depend on relative prices; and, in a free system, relative prices depend, not only on demand but also upon the number of people offering their services. Only if such numbers are determined in advance and the emoluments attached to them fixed by authority can this factor be neglected.

It seems, therefore, that in changing conditions and in the absence of total control of permitted recruitment, the more detailed the manpower plan and the more specialised the training, the more likely it is to be wrong than right. The wider the categories and the greater the degree of the cultivation of versatility, the greater the potential response to unforeseen change, both in demand and supply. A further education in the broad principles of science and technology, at least until the last stages of training for high expert competence, is far better suited to meet the 'needs' of society than minute specialisation with narrow limits on the volume of admission permitted.

But if this is so it points away from the policy of detailed manpower planning in favour of admission to the various sections of higher and further education on the basis of general tests of ability and willingness to benefit – the Liberal rather than the Totalitarian principle. Needless to say this does not imply indifference to probable trends of willingness to enter upon various kinds of training on the part of applicants for higher education or the likely openings at various starting income levels in different fields of employment. But it does mean that, given any informal guidance which it may seem sensible to provide, the ultimate choice lies with the would-be student who, in some way or other, has satisfied the minimal capacity and that to make available places for persons who satisfy these criteria becomes the main preoccupation of policy.

INDIGENCE AND DISTRESS

I now turn to the relief of indigence and distress. In detail this involves a host of very complex problems – legal, administrative and economic; and the history of policy in this respect is a subject in itself. Here it is possible only to deal with the broadest aspects of principle.

At the outset we may recognise explicitly the general case for measures of this sort. There may still be those who argue that there is no public obligation in this respect: that the individual should be responsible for making provision against all possible contingencies for himself and his family and that, beyond that, all relief should be left to spontaneous private charity. But, stated overtly, this is a minority view. Although the assumption by the state, or its organs, of the functions of eleemosynary relief certainly introduces all sorts of problems with no easy solution, it is doubtful whether, in Western societies today, many would positively oppose it. Employment opportunities may shrink, personal disasters may occur in the form of accidents and ill-health, old people and children may be the victims of other people's negligence; and, in such contingencies, private charity may easily not be sufficient to avert situations which evoke a demand that not all relief be left to the generous and warm-hearted.

The attitude of the Classical Economists in this respect has been much misunderstood and misrepresented. It is true that Malthus and Ricardo, prepossessed with the dangers of population increase and shocked by the effects of the policies which had become prevalent under the old Poor Laws, urged the gradual cessation of all such relief. But the main Classical position as laid down by Senior, the author of the Report of the early 1830s and accepted by most of his contemporaries among economists, was otherwise. According to his *Letter to*

Lord Howick,* the great test which must be applied to any project of state action in regard to relief is the question *whether it has any tendency to increase that which it is proposed to relieve.* This is very important; it makes explicit the dominating principle underlying the general Classical attitude. 'As far as the poor are concerned', he says, 'to make the supply of relief adequate to the demand for it; and, as far as the rich are concerned, to apportion equally the burthen of affording that relief . . . these are noble purposes, and as far as they can be effected without materially diminishing industry, forethought and charity, it is the imperious duty of Government to effect them.'

Thus he is all in favour of provision for the blind, the insane, the chronic invalid and the maimed.

No public fund for the relief of these calamities has any tendency to diminish industry or providence. They are evils too great to allow individuals to make any sufficient provision against them, and too rare to be, in fact, provided against by them at all. Their permanency, too, is likely to weary out private sympathy. And the worst of them, madness, is perhaps the calamity with which we least adequately sympathise. Even to educated persons the insane are too frequently objects of aversion. I wish, therefore, to see these evils met by an ample compulsory provision.

For the same reason, he favoured public provision of medical treatment, the erection, regulation and support of fever hospitals, infirmaries and dispensaries. He also believed that there is a case for public provision for orphans. But he opposed special provision for old age.†

These are far-reaching positive proposals and may well be claimed as anticipating more recent thought in this connection. The great difference between Senior's position and that of our own day was in regard to the relief of the able-bodied and their dependents. Here there was no question of abolishing relief. But there was firm insistence on the famous *Principle of Less Eligibility,* namely the principle that the relief given must be limited to an amount which leaves the position of the relieved

---

*Nassau Senior, *Letter to Lord Howick,* p. 14.

†From Senior's point of view the needs of old age came into the category of the relief of general indigence.

inferior to that of the position of the employed and their dependents. This on two grounds. First, that if assistance was an unconditional right and there was no upper limit to its level, there was an encouragement to improvident marriage, and, secondly, because of its alleged effect on the character and initiative of the recipient. It was felt too that the laws of settlement which were an integral part of the prevailing system of local rather than national relief, hindered the mobility of labourers and perpetuated unemployment which otherwise would not have occurred.

So far so good. Nowadays the laws of settlement would find no defenders in free societies – at any rate *within* national boundaries. As for the *Principle of Less Eligibility*, although ideas relating to the scope of its application may have changed, few would deny the logic on which it rests or the desirability of its observance in many connections. If a person is paid more by way of relief, or even nearly as much, than he or she can earn by working, the incentive to work is likely to be considerably weakened. It is true that if the receipt of relief carries with it some sort of disapprobation, this tendency to some extent may be offset. But the presumption remains that the nearer relief approaches the return to effort, the greater the danger of disincentive. The trouble about the classical prescriptions for the able-bodied and their dependents lay not in this principle but in the relief of its application in the form of the workhouse.

Now it is perfectly true that that workhouse as realised by the practice of the Poor Law Commissioners differed in important respects from the recommendations of Senior and his associates;* the general mixing up of the able-bodied and the old and children was the reverse of what they had contemplated. But workhouse relief *per se* was open to serious criticism. It was relief given in circumstances which were almost bound to involve, both for the applicants and to the world at large, a penumbra of social stigma. It was relief in kind, carrying with it the implication that the recipients were incapable of a prudent disposal of cash. It was relief obtainable only by quitting the home and entering an institution. It is not necessary to disbelieve in the real evils of the old Poor Laws with their disregard

*On the detail of all this, the able analysis of Professor Marion Bowley's *Nassau Senior and Classical Economics* (London: Allen & Unwin, 1937) pt ii, ch. 2 should be consulted.

of the Principle of Less Eligibility to judge the workhouse test to have been too strong a reaction to that earlier situation. The able-bodied who with their dependents were to be denied relief, save on these terms, may well have included vagrants and persons demoralised by indiscriminate public assistance. But they also included persons willing to work, dislodged by economic change and fluctuation, and lacking adequate resources to bridge the interval before re-employment. It is legitimate criticism of the authors of the principles of 1834 that they tended to ignore the difficulty for those with lower incomes of accumulating in advance sufficient to meet the various misfortunes to which they might be exposed. It is therefore not surprising that developments since their day have taken other and less stringent directions. The present apparatus of social security in the United Kingdom with its pensions, provision for ill-health and unemployment and supplementary benefits would certainly surprise the thinkers of the Classical period. They might have endorsed most of the aims but in all probability they would have had, at any rate, residual doubts about some of the methods.

Whether this is so or not, it is clear that present arrangements and the rules which they involve are not immune from criticism on grounds of general principle. On the plane of generality, on which we are now moving, we may mention two broad problems arising in this connection: the problem of compulsory insurance and the problem of a means test.

So far as insurance is concerned, there can be no objection from the libertarian point of view to some form of compulsion. Few would call in question the desirability of compulsory insurance against automobile accidents to third parties or industrial accidents to employees; and since accidents and ill-health and loss of employment are only too apt to involve burdens on others, it is at least arguable that it is no offence against liberty to compel some provision against these contingencies. Clearly there are some arguments against this point of view which, however, diminish in cogency in so far as there are dependents not otherwise provided for. It may be urged that a single man should be left to choose whether or not to run the risk of ill-health and starvation just as, according to civilised standards, he may choose whether or not to commit suicide: the argument for compulsion here rests upon the extent to which his choice involves positive nuisance to others. But while admitting the possibility of reasonables differences of opinion on such cases, I see no important infringement of the principles of freedom in the imposition of obligations of this sort.

Where there must be more controversy in this connection is when, as is usually the case, the compulsion extends to contributions from employers and is made to what is called an 'insurance fund' seldom managed on strict insurance principles, and certainly involving subsidy at once from the tax on employment and from the general state contribution. Here there is considerable dispute concerning both the direction of the contribution and the degree of supplementation by taxation. The opponents of social insurance in this form may not object to compulsory insurance as such, but they certainly argue that here, as with other forms of insurance, the individual should be left to make his own arrangements. They argue further that such arrangements are financed less by transfers between higher and lower groups and far more by levies whose incidence is ultimately *within the main groups* insured; and that they thus involve subtractions which the persons concerned might well be left to dispose of individually. It is contended therefore that a community which has attained what, in a former age, would have been regarded as middle-class standards of living, might well be left, subject to the general principle of compulsion, to make arrangements which persons in the middle and higher income group have long been expected to do for themselves.

Where genuine insurance is concerned there is naturally no question of a means test. But where it is a question of relief pure and simple, or insurance subsidised by the taxpayer, then the arguments for ascertainment of genuine need are very cogent. Why, for instance, should a well-to-do person be subsidised by the state on grounds of age or ill-health simply because he is a citizen? Is there not an entirely unnecessary degree of taxation if universal benefits are to be accessible? Is it not much more consistent with our ideas of personal liberty that, subject to any compulsion to make minimum provision for certain contingencies and to contribute to general taxation, the citizen should be entitled to subsidy only on proof of inability to pay?

Yet the means test as it has been practised in the past is subject to obvious disadvantages. It involves special enquiries which are resented and may therefore give rise to deception. And it is a disincentive to work and saving, if, so soon as additional income is earned, the relief hitherto available automatically disappears. Anomalies in this respect are especially conspicuous if those who continue to work past a retiring age are subject to a suspension of state pensions.

In recent times the suggestion has been made that such difficulties (and many others) would automatically disappear if, for the whole ungainly corpus of present-day relief and security arrangements, there were substituted the principle of negative income taxation, or 'tax credits' as it is sometimes called. The state could fix a minimum, consistent with the general principle of less eligibility, below which no income tax should be paid but, instead, payments compensatory of the difference from the minimum should be given. The existing revenue arrangements would indicate when means were insufficient and eligibility for relief established; and, in calculating the degree of entitlement, adequate allowance could be given for various defined burdens and contingencies. A whole apparatus of administration and supervision would be rendered unnecessary: and there would come into being a mechanism for the automatic alleviation of poverty consistent with self-respect on the part of the beneficiaries and not dependent on private goodwill.

RELIEF AND THE POPULATION PROBLEM

There is one difficulty about all such solutions to the relief problem which, although it may not be inevitable, is yet sufficiently important to deserve separate mention: I refer to their possible effects on the growth of population.

This is essentially a question of whether the relief offered may not increase the problem it is designed to alleviate. For, although the causal relationships are complex, it is difficult to believe that there may not be some connection between automatic provision for children and the size of families; and, having regard to the imminent threat to happiness which arises from the population explosion of our day, it is surely unwise to ignore this possibility. Fears of this sort undoubtedly influenced to some extent the Classical attitude to the problems of relief in general.

I use the word 'possibility' in this connection deliberately. It is obviously not certain that provision for children, either by way of tax relief or by way of cash subventions, will necessarily affect the size of families. There was a time indeed, at the outset of the discussion of family allowances, when it was argued that no such influence need be feared. Once a certain level of income has been achieved in communities not subject to taboos regarding birth control, it is certainly arguable that the prospect of additional cash per additional child might be counterbalanced by other influences. Indeed it is conceivable that other influences tending to a damaging decline in population might positively need offsetting by increased cash allowances. But there are still many parts of the world where this is not so – where the increase of population bids fair to outweigh the best efforts of accumulation and invention, where, therefore, relief from the pressure on resources due to large families would be most desirable. Demographers often make mistakes, but it is difficult to believe that in such parts the devil of Malthus shows any sign of being chained.

What then is to be done. Next to the possibility of nuclear warfare, the population explosion of our day is the main menace to the future of the race. Yet to visit the punishment for indiscriminate propagation on the children is repugnant to a sense of humanity. What is needed eventually is a wholesale change in the attitude to large families: the widest availability of methods of preventing them and the exposure as a gross offence against fundamental ethical principle of those creeds which deprecate their use. For the hundreds of millions unable to count beyond ten, a prime *desideratum* would be some sort of oral contraceptive at least as attractive as alcohol or tobacco. But, in the meantime in those areas where the menace of excessive natality is greatest, I confess that I view with great apprehension any free cash reliefs to families larger than sufficient to maintain a constant population. Beyond that point I regard it as preferable that relief should be in kind or in vouchers of limited exchangeability – at any rate until the present demographic tendencies have altered radically.

INDISCRIMINATE BENEFIT

Finally, in any view of the provision of welfare, we must not neglect to take into account all those activities, usually the result of action by the state, which afford indiscriminate benefit – parks, roads, proper regulation of the lay-out and sky-line of cities, the prevention of pollution, and so on. At an earlier stage in the argument I have already stressed the importance of such activities. In this context it needs only to be pointed out that, on any valid technique of estimating the distribution of the means of welfare, their availability must be regarded as tending to diminish inequality.

CHAPTER 9

Collectivism

INTRODUCTION: MATTERS OF NOMENCLATURE

The points of view which I have developed in the preceding chapters are not in all respects similar to the various theories of economic policy in Classical Political Economy. But I hope they are not in radical disharmony with the spirit of that system which I regard as an important contribution to the Liberal philosophy of society to which I adhere.

At the period when these principles were promulgated there seemed to be some hope that this influence would eventually become general; and, given the inevitable differences of the heritage of history in different parts of the world, that they would be adopted as a background setting for further development. To some extent that expectation has been fulfilled. In many areas much, although not all, of the ethos of the System of Economic Freedom has prevailed; and some would say it has played its part in the unprecedented advances in the standard of life of the inhabitants which has been characteristic of the last two centuries. But this ascendancy has not been general. In large parts of the world what there was of Economic Liberalism has been supplanted by Totalitarian Communism; and in many others elsewhere it is not untrue to say that the principles on which it rests are under attack. If we are candid with ourselves it must be admitted that much of the contemporary thought concerning the future organisation of society would describe itself as tending towards Collectivism rather than anything which can be called Liberal in the traditional sense of the word. It is worthwhile, therefore, devoting some little time to the examination of this attitude and its implications.

To some extent the contrast is semantic rather than substantial. As I have emphasised already, the conception of Classical Liberalism assumed as part of its outlook a great deal of organisation which must necessarily be described as Collectivist. All those services which, in Adam Smith's classic phrase, it could not be to the interest of any individual or small group of individuals to provide with a profit, that is to say the apparatus of law and order, the so-called infrastructure of roads, harbours, water supply, sewage disposal and so on and so forth, can certainly be described as Collectivist. If writers propounding the theories of policy of the Classical tradition choose to describe the total system as Individualist, they have only themselves to blame if it is pointed out to them that a substantial part of what they would at once admit to be economic structure is of essentially Collectivist in this sense.

Somewhat similar considerations could well be applied to much of the underpinning of the distribution of income provided by modern states. Although, as I have pointed out in my last two chapters, it is arguable that some at any rate of the relief or support now provided in kind, free schooling for instance, might well be provided in cash and thus permit more individualism in choice, it is undeniable that the provision of the funds for this group of services is provided by governmental authority levying rates and taxes and, equally with the apparatus of law and order and the infrastructure, can also be described as Collectivist. Thus an individualist, who wished to get credit or gain argumentative advantage in debate with opponents, might say that he was Collectivist in this respect; and a Collectivist, wishing to gain support for other kinds of Collectivist organisation, might point to the common agreement as to the desirability of services of this kind as an argument for Collectivism in general. The Webbs did a good deal of this.

But all this would be a battle about words. As we have seen, the provision of services and welfare of the kind under discussion was urged, in greater or lesser degree, by the Classical Economists themselves; and although there is plenty of scope for argument about particular forms of policy and regulation in these spheres, it is *not* the real argument between Collectivism and Non-collectivism. That argument relates essentially to the sphere where, within an appropriate setting of law, spontaneous initiatives and relationships can arise and have indeed existed in one form or another and in greater or lesser degree in most areas during the greater part of recorded history. Are the non-indivisible means of production, the means of production capable of use by individuals or groups of individuals, to be collectively owned and managed, or is their ownership to be diffused in private or corporate hands whose activities are guided wholly or in greater part by the impersonal forces of the market? Is economic activity in general to be planned from the centre and guided by directives from the centre; or is it to be a system of decentralised initiative whose ultimate control is the demand of consumers and investors? This is the essential problem of Collectivism *versus* the System of Economic Freedom; and it is to this problem that I wish to direct attention in this chapter.

PARTIAL COLLECTIVISM

We may begin by considering the Collectivist elements in the so-called mixed economy.

It will be remembered that when I spoke of the monopoly problem in the free economy I pointed out that, where the technical conditions of production involved monopoly, as in the case of pipelines or transport tracks involving compulsory purchase powers, there was at least a problem of regulation – the so-called public-utility problem – and that this might be met either by special franchises or perhaps by outright public ownership and control. If the latter alternative is adopted, then there is clearly an island or series of islands of Collectivism in an otherwise sea of private enterprise. The same phenomenon may arise when, for ideological reasons, industrial groups quite capable of existing with a fair degree of competition are nationalised – the steel industry, for instance, in the United Kingdom.

Now no one in his senses would argue that such mixed systems cannot exist – they do over a considerable area in many parts of the other free-enterprise world – or that they are necessarily unstable. Sometimes the spectacle of nationalised industry seems to excite people to want more; sometimes it has the contrary effect. For reasons which I shall develop, I personally am inclined to think that the less of this sort of thing the better. But I would dissociate myself from those who predict the end of the world because, for instance, for better or worse, the postal and telegraph industries are nationalised.

Nevertheless in my judgement there are disadvantages in this form of organisation, and the more it prevails the more widely they will show themselves.

First, if they are both owned *and managed* from the centre they tend to be wooden and unadaptable to change. It is not easy for the best executive mind to function at its best in a situation liable to parliamentary question and therefore requiring written reasons for all but the most minor decisions.

This disadvantage has long been recognised by moderate Collectivists. The remedy which has been adopted is the creation of the Public Board – for example the Coal Board, the Railway Board, and so on; and it has become a convention that the detail of their conduct of business is not a matter for parliamentary question. This gives some freedom in respect of detail. But it does not eliminate an extraordinary waste of time in negotiations regarding general questions of policy between the chief executives and the government departments which are supposed to supervise them. At the same time it also renders popular control more difficult. If something goes wrong, if arbitrary decisions are taken, it is extremely difficult for the ordinary citizen, as distinct from the bureaucrats, to do anything about it. You create, as it were, independent feudal baronies owing allegiance to the state and indeed controlled in matters of major policy, but far less susceptible of control, in matters smaller than this, than corporations having limited franchises which may be taken away if the original terms of the lease are infringed.

But beyond this there are more serious disadvantages. Nationalised industry is almost inevitably mixed up in politics; and the pace of expansion and contraction – matters of major policy – is much more likely to depend on political decisions than on responses to the pressures of the market. The price policy of such undertakings is liable to be determined by political considerations. Moreover, and even more significant, the fact that it is the property of the state releases it from the ultimate market control of inefficiency: it cannot go bankrupt.

This means that the spur to normal efficiency is blunted and – what is more serious – there is no upper limit to what can be forced from it by way of wage demands. If the ordinary private corporation is faced with demands which go beyond a certain point, it can always tell its opposite number at the conference table that it may be forced to close down. But that argument is less persuasive from the heads of public boards; the taxpayer is assumed to be able to foot the bill: and, as we have already seen, that may well be a menace to the stability of the whole system.

For these reasons, as I said in an earlier chapter, where monopoly is technically inevitable I incline to the regulated corporation solution rather than outright collective ownership. Each alternative has its difficulties. But I think experience shows that those of the latter are much more formidable than those of the former.

TOTAL COLLECTIVISM: THE CLASSICAL ATTITUDE

I now come to Total Collectivism, the Mecca of Communist ideology and the system which actually prevails in Soviet Russia and the Iron Curtain countries, the system in which the means of production, distribution and exchange are wholly owned and directed by government authority.

Now there can be no doubt at all that this would have been rejected root and branch by the main body of the Classical Economists. There is no systematic discussion thereof in the literature. But the *obiter dicta*, which I have discussed at length in an earlier work,* make it quite clear that they would have regarded it as detrimental, both to productive efficiency and to personal liberty. It was something totally opposed to their conception of a sensible and ethically acceptable organisation of economic activity.

The exception to this is the position of John Stuart Mill who is sometimes claimed as supporter of the Collectivist attitude. And it is quite true that in the *Autobiography* he speaks of himself and his wife becoming more and more willing to describe themselves as socialists. It is true too that, in the third edition of his *Principles*, the discussion of certain socialist proposals

*In *Theory of Economic Policy in English Classical Political Economy*, ch. IV.

which, in earlier editions, had lent themselves to an anti-
socialist interpretation, contained much which *prima facie*
might be thought to be support of a genuinely Collectivist
position.

But this claim does not stand up to serious scrutiny. In any
discussion of Mill's attitude in this respect, the propositions of
his *On Liberty*, which he regarded as being of all his works the
most valuable and likely to last, are to be regarded as crucial;
and there we find it very clearly stated that

> If the roads and railways, the banks, the insurance com-
> panies, the great joint stock companies, the universities and
> the public charities were all of them branches of the govern-
> ment, if in addition the municipal corporations and local
> boards became departments of the central administration, if
> the employees of all these different enterprises were appointed
> and paid for by the government and looked to the govern-
> ment for every rise in life, not all the freedom of the press and
> popular constitution of the legislature would make this or
> any other country free otherwise than in name.*

Few statements could be less equivocal than that.

In fact, if Mill's position is examined in detail, particularly
in regard to his chapter on the 'Probable Future of the
Labouring Classes', which I have done elsewhere,† it will be
found that his 'Socialism', such as it was, consisted largely in
hopes for the future of worker co-operatives and a plea for the
sympathetic consideration of the possibility of experiments of
the kind suggested by Fourier – the very opposite of Total
Collectivism whose supporters of the First International he
condemned in the strongest terms. On the whole, subsequent
experience has not hitherto given much support to Mill's hopes
in such connections: the success of worker co-operatives has
been very limited.‡ But one thing is quite certain, Mill was
never a supporter of Total Collectivism and would have loathed
it in its present manifestations.

On Liberty, pp. 168–9.
† *Theory of Economic Policy in English Classical Political Economy*, ch. v.
‡I have been inspired and impressed by what I have seen of the Kibutzim in
Israel. But I think there are special reasons which prevent them being regarded as
typical.

TOTAL COLLECTIVISM: DISTRIBUTION AND INCENTIVE

Since, therefore, systematic discussion of this matter is absent from the Classical System, we must survey the subject from the point of view of more recent theoretical speculation and practical experience. We may do this under the three heads of distribution and incentive, production and allocation, and general political implications.

To begin with distribution and incentive. One of the main arguments for Collectivism has been the abolition of inequality; and it must be freely granted that if private ownership of the means of production is prohibited, inequality of income and wealth – as distinct from power – from that source is *ipso facto* absent. But as far as income from work is concerned, the possibilities are still open. So far as I know the Marxian prescription for ultimate justice – from each according to his ability, to each according to his needs – has never yet been attempted in Communist countries; and the obvious difficulties of determining needs in a wide sense suggest that such an attempt is unlikely – the system in so-called Capitalist societies of progressive income taxes and relief for clearly defined needs seems to deserve more credit on this score than generalised formulae. But equality as between adult workers is clearly not administratively impossible; and, at an early stage in the Russian Revolution, it seems actually to have been tried.

Unfortunately (or fortunately) such a system presents great difficulties in practice. In a completely stationary state it would certainly diminish the incentive to work in many branches of activity. Of course, as has been said already, for artists, some academics and political reformers, the pecuniary incentive may well be secondary. If you are on the brink of a great scientific discovery or the achievement of some social innovation which you think will change the lot of great numbers of people, the cash incentive may be negligible. But the ordinary work of the world cannot be said to be like this; and if it makes no difference whether you work hard or not, the probability is that, on balance, the amount done will be less. Moreover, in changing conditions, if there are no differences between rewards in activities where the need for labour is increasing and those activities where it is declining, then obviously the necessary adaptation will not take place spontaneously and coercive direction will be necessary.

All this is no figment of the reactionary imagination. The experience of Soviet Russia is there to verify this argument. As all the world knows, it was found necessary in that area to reintroduce differences of pay as an incentive to labour; and my own impression is that, if incomes are reckoned net of taxes and benefits in kind – cars, *dachas* and so on – are counted in, the degree of inequality of income from work in that country is certainly not visibly different from that prevailing elsewhere – to put it very cautiously. Where difference in power over other people is concerned, the difference in the United Kingdom between the position of Mr Wilson or Mr Heath on the one hand, and an ordinary factory worker on the other, is certainly much less than the difference in this regard between Mr Brezhnev and Mr Kosygin and a Russian worker similarly placed. It should go without saying that, in a one-party system, the inequality of opportunity for promotion and the sweets of office are far greater than elsewhere.

As for incentive to move between different areas and industries, it is notorious that the Russian system, even with its differentials, involves direction of labour as in an army. In that unhappy country you cannot move *internally* without a passport and changing jobs is a matter of strict regulation.

TOTAL COLLECTIVISM: PRODUCTION AND ALLOCATION

All this is relatively non-controversial. Even Mill, who bent over backwards to discover possibilities of the working of non-pecuniary incentives in what Marx called the 'duo-decimo editions of the New Jerusalem' which he discussed, had to admit that the human race would have to reach new levels of enlightenment before such possibilities could be achieved. As I have argued earlier, Alfred Marshall was surely incontestably right when he emphasised the importance of the common and *strongest* motives rather than the *highest* in building the basis of a stable society.

Much more debatable is the question of the possibilities of planning Collectivist production in such a way as to respond to commonly accepted social *desiderata* – the problem of the allocation of productive services under a system in which there are no markets for capital or productive services.

Strange to relate it was not until this century that this problem received serious attention. There is a passing reference in a review by Mill* which shows that he had not appreciated the nature of the difficulty; and in so far as the Marxian literature shows any awareness of the problem – which, since Marx himself discouraged speculation about the arrangements of the future, was not much – it assumed that labour costs would provide an appropriate planning instrument – an assumption which, apart from ignoring differences of skill, evades the whole capital problem and the problem of scarce natural resources.† It was not until the early 1920s that the problem attracted wide attention when von Mises, the Austrian economist, in his famous work on Socialism, *Die Gemeinwirtschaft*, boldly asserted that economic calculation would be out of the question in communities where there existed no markets in services and other means of production and that therefore, in such conditions, rational production would be impossible (*unmöglich*).

As might be expected, this contention aroused much debate. The fact of the problem was recognised by the more responsible Socialist thnkers: Oscar Lange, who had a solution of his own, said, half seriously, half sarcastically, that in the Socialist state of the future there should be a monument to von Mises for having drawn attention to it. But its insolubility was denied, and various solutions were suggested. Speaking broadly these fell into two groups. Either they rested upon hitherto neglected models by Pareto and Barone (which incidentally seem precisely to show the very great practical difficulties of the problem). Or they involved proposals for a *simulation* of markets

---

*Mill, *Essays in Economics and Society*, pp. 439–57.

†Thus, in pure labour-cost planning, an oak tree which took a hundred years to come to maturity would be counted as equivalent to a conifer which matured in less than half that number of years, if each took the same time in planting and cutting; and a machine involving steel pivots would be regarded, for planning purposes as equivalent to one involving diamonds, if the labour costs were the same.

by decentralised units, playing, so to speak, as if real competition existed. And because some of their authors, conspicuously Lange and Lerner, were men of great ability and persuasive power the impression has become diffused that the von Mises proposition has been shown to be without foundation.

Now impossible *(unmöglich)* is a strong word; and I have no doubt at all that von Mises deprived his position of much of its force by using it. It is true that he was using it in regard to what he called rational production, production which responded as nearly as possible to the demands of consumers and investors as the nature of activity in a world of uncertainty would permit. But be that as it may, the use of such a word in a world in which Collectivist systems were churning out vast quantities of stuff which, whether or not it corresponded to the von Mises ideal of rationality, had *some* use for *some* purposes, was bound to give rise to scepticism. This was a pity because there is much more substance in the von Mises position than is usually supposed.

As I see it the essential position is as follows. There can be no question that, in a situation such as a major war, a centrally planned economy whose output has some rational significance is both conceivable and practically possible. The aim is simple: to win the war. The essential problem is therefore to produce for domestic consumption in terms of food, clothing and so on the minimum means necessary to sustain morale and health for the non-military population – quantities which to some extent can be *technically* estimated – leaving all the rest of the productive potential for the war effort. Doubtless there are profound problems arising from scarcities of materials and services even here; and the use of markets and prices in special sectors may be desirable. But the nature of the aims and the urgencies of the situation make the very idea of running a major war by the price mechanism alone a little ridiculous.

Similar possibilities exist in dictatorial systems where those in power place certain *technically defined* operations as the prime objectives of policy and are prepared, more or less, to let the rest go hang. It is clearly not impossible to command the erection of steel works and munition factories, and, given that they are afforded absolute priority in recruitment of labour and supply of materials, to get the programme executed. I am convinced that much of the history of the Russian economy, both before and after the war, is to be explained in these terms.* The evolution of Soviet industry before the Second World War is surely best understood in the light of the determination, not necessarily to be condemned, to build up the industrial infrastructure of a *defence* economy; and the great technical successes since then in the sphere of space travel and nuclear research are also to be explained in terms of shock tactics, not unconnected with military policy – concentrating effort on specific technical objectives rather than any strong effort to respond to the desire for consumption and the time-preferences of the ordinary citizen. I do not think that any good purpose can be served by describing such operations as impossible. They have clearly taken place.

The trouble arises, and the real significance of the von Mises analysis emerges, when the range of objectives widens and it is no longer a question of quantities technically defined, but rather a deployment of resources so as, in some sense or other, to equalise the values produced at a variety of margins to minister to a great variety of demands. Here the absence of market mechanisms for the pricing of productive services and the lack of direction of resources according to the criterion of profitability seems bound to produce confusion. To organise a system of such flexibility as is needed to produce efficiency in such a context seems to involve so great a degree of decentralisation and independent initiative as to burst, as it were, the conception of centralised planning. The Lerner idea of decentralised units all playing at competition could only be realised if the managers had the choice of what products to produce and in what number, and the scope to reinvest working capital in new lines, and to sell what fixed capital seemed superfluous. I think it is no accident that all such experiments in the Iron Curtain countries have led either to the overthrow of the government attempting them, as in Czechoslovakia, or in a recoil to greater control from the centre – the negation of responses to the variegated demands of consumers and their systems of time-preference.

*I have developed this position at some length in my *Economic Problems in Peace and War*, ch. II.

TOTAL COLLECTIVISM AND LIBERTY

This brings me to the last point which I wish to bring out in this connection – the incompatibility of Total Collectivism with liberty, not only in the limited sense of liberty in consumption and in movement, but also in the wider political and social sense.

The difficulties of operating a Collectivist system in the virtually necessary absence of meaningful markets and independent initiative seem to lead to a general tendency to adapt the people to the plan rather than the plan to the people. And this in time surely leads to a tendency to limit freedom of discussion, criticism of those in authority, and eventually to physical restraints on those who dare to infringe these limitations. Doubtless some of the horrors of the Stalinist regime should be viewed in the context of Russian history where political liberty has always been at a discount and where cruelty and oppression have tended to be regarded as naturally inevitable – though it is to be noted that, in all probability, Stalin killed or exiled more millions than all previous Russian rulers put together. But while much can be attributed to historical tradition and individual wickedness, it is surely superficial to leave it at that. If the analysis which I have been developing has validity then, given the Total Collectivist objective, there is something in the logic of action itself which must lead in greater or lesser degree to a much greater curtailment of the liberties of the ordinary citizen than is probable under less-centralised regimes.

Whether you regard that as a recommendation, whether you welcome the limitations of speculative thought, the regimentation of ignorant opinion by shy-making slogans and the cultivation of hero-worship by ubiquitous giant photographs and a popular shrine, comparable to the most naïve excesses of earlier superstitions, is of course a matter of ultimate values. I do not. For me it is a degradation of the type 'man'.

SYNDICALISM AND GUILD SOCIALISM

It may help to clarify the nature of the choices now confronting contemporary society if we consider briefly two variants of the revolutionary substitute for the Liberal System alternative to Communism, namely Syndicalism and its British watered-down version Guild Socialism.

Popular interpretation of the history of revolutionary movements often regards the Syndicalist outlook as similar to that of Communism proper; and it is true that where agitation against the historic status quo has taken place, its protagonists have often fought or demonstrated side by side, although not without minor quarrels among themselves as regards tactics and jargon. But in fact, as we shall see, they are fundamentally different. They may share a common opposition to the System of Economic Freedom and its supporting conceptions of the functions of the state. They may subscribe to the fashionable analysis of the so-called bourgeois mentality. They may combine, in demonstrations or even violence, against established institutions. But, in ultimate objectives, Syndicalism and Communism are at opposite ends of the pole. Communism, that is Total Collectivism, proposed a society unified by central control and central planning – any degree of decentralisation allowed is instrumental. As opposed to this, Syndicalism, in its pure form, proposes a totally non-centralised economy, the various productive enterprises being owned and managed by associations of producers, 'democratically' controlled in the sense that the workers concerned have the same sort of ultimate rights as members of French *syndicats* or British trade unions, but masters *vis-à-vis* the rest of the economy as regards policy and services.

Now there are obvious difficulties as regards this conception – at least as soon as it is generalised as a system applicable to the whole, or nearly the whole, of a large community. As the formidable Beatrice Webb, one of the joint founders of Fabian Socialism, is said to have remarked, 'the Railways for the Railwaymen, perhaps . . . but what about the Sewers for the Sewagemen?' The idea of a neat pattern of clearly defined associations of producers each performing functions which would complement, rather than overlap with, each other was something which could only occur to literary exhibitionists, such as Georges Sorel, rather than to anyone who had the slightest acquaintance with the complexities of a modern industrial society. Certainly there can be industrial unions, recruiting their members from a variety of productive enterprises; but any belief that, say, the Transport and General Workers' Union could function in this way, and be the management of the unheard-of conglomerate which it would thus cover, does not stand up to serious examination.

But the main difficulties of syndicalism are not definitional or classificatory: they are difficulties which go to the heart of the main economic problems of society.

First there are problems of personal recruitment and transfer. If the syndicates are owners of the capital at their disposal, we may assume that, like all monopolistic bodies in history, they will be very jealous of recruitment. As with some of the more powerful craft trade unions of our day, there will be a strong hereditary element in admission and in any case, as with certain professions, there will be obstacles in the shape of so-called professional or apprenticeship requirements totally out of harmony with technical necessities. It is not at all easy to see how a total Syndicalist society would arrange for the employ-ment of the potential working population. But, supposing that problem not to exist, there would still be further problems as regards transfer. Suppose a man wished to leave his syndicate, would he or would he not be permitted to take with him a proportionate share of the capital? If the latter alternative prevailed, there would be an obvious impediment to mobility; if the former an additional complication in capital planning.

But this leads to a more general consideration. It is the main claim of Communism, as regards organisation of production, that it allows a consistent allocation of resources in general according to a single plan. Earlier this chapter I argued that, save where military or quasi-military allocations are involved, such claims are likely to be without foundation and that, in the absence of the decentralised initiatives of disbursed property and the market, the wishes of the citizens are more likely to be sacrificed to the plan than the plan adapted to their wishes. But under pure Syndicalism, not even the claim of rational allocation could be justified. With the total absence of co-ordi-nation either from the centre or from competitive markets, the idea of any tendency to organisation tending to roughly equal returns and costs at various margins would be nonsensical. It would be a nightmare of uncontrolled monopolies, each seeking to maximise its gains at the expense of the others. It may well be argued that the System of Economic Freedom, so far as it has been historically realised, with its state-fostered immobilities and monopolistic positions, fails in all sorts of ways to conform to the claims which may be made for its ideal type. But any falling short here pales into insignificance before the total chaos which is implicit in the conception of unrestricted Syndicalism – a non-stop economic war of each group against all others.

It was some realisation of such potentialities which led to the compromise between pure Syndicalism and pure Collectivism which was suggested in the 1920s and 1930s by the British Guild Socialists. Let the management and control of the various productive organisations be in the hands of those employed in them, as under Syndicalism it was suggested, but let the ownership of the means of production be in the hands of the state. In this way, it was urged that the obvious objections to pure Syndicalism could be circumnavigated and its release of the soul for organised groups of producers be retained.

At first sight the compromise seems attractive: at the time of its promulgation it inspired much interest. But closer examination, not so much by professional economists as by the Guild Socialists themselves, revealed difficulties. The main economic problem in the sphere of production is the allocation problem. Organisation within groups is important as regards technical efficiency and morale. But the outstanding problem is that of the proportion of resources to be devoted to the different productive services; and this is not a problem which the management of each group can solve for itself. In the absence of markets, therefore, the state as provider of capital and ultimate owner must play a very positive role. But what if the state and the National Guilds, as they were called, do not agree? If this happens, as is not unlikely, the idea of freedom from the distasteful conception of centralised power and all that that involves disappears. Endless debates on this problem took place in the inner circles – the works of Cole, the high priest of the movement, are littered with such discussions. Could there be some body, not called the state, which should mediate between the state and the Guilds in the event of disagreement? And so

F

on and so forth. Eventually the movement petered out in an absurd tangle of co-ordinating committees without, so far as I know, any reference to the possibility of uses of a price mechanism; and even its devotees gave it up and returned to something like the Fabian Collectivism which it had been supposed to supersede with perhaps some greater emphasis on what is called worker participation – a concept which has yet to be clarified.

Nowadays I venture to think it is easier to see this episode in a clearer, more practical perspective and to realise that, far from solving the contradictions of Collectivism and Syndicalism, in a way it combined their worst features. The consolidation of management into gigantic monopolistic groups, in so far as it was given freedom, made the allocation problem more difficult; and the fact that the ultimate responsibility for the capital resources was in the hands of the state was almost bound to give rise to the illusion of the bottomless purse which we know so well and its accompaniment of financial irresponsibility. It is possible to argue that Total Collectivism, with its limitless power of control over the lives of its citizens, can perhaps avoid instability, at any rate in the value of money. The conception of the original Guild Socialists seems to create a state of affairs in which inflation always seems the easy way out.

CHAPTER 10

International Economic Relations

INTRODUCTION

In my discussion hitherto I have been examining problems of political economy as if there were one supreme body concerned with public policy and one only, all complications of international economic (and political) relations being left on one side. In fact, however, on the unfortunate planet on which we live there is more than one such body; and some of the most anxious questions of policy arise from this circumstance. I propose therefore to devote this chapter to a survey of these questions. These are matters on which political economists of the earlier Classical tradition did some of their most interesting and valuable work. But they are also matters on which their thought was nevertheless incomplete and on which the changing circumstances of the world have opened up new vistas of problems and attempted solutions.

NATURE OF THE PROBLEM

Let us begin by reminding ourselves of the essential nature of the problem. The inhabitants of this world are not governed by one authority. For good or for bad the coercive element in society is organised by a substantial number of separate sovereign states, some large and influential, some less so and some not mattering a bit, but, in the past at any rate, all claiming independence, equal voting power in the Assembly of the United Nations, and ultimate power of initiative in all matters relating to law, defence and administration. Thus while direct relations between these bodies are governed by treaties, alliances and sometimes even by non-sovereign supranational organisations, there is no coercive common authority over all. We need not enquire here what forces of social cohesion – or terror – maintain this state of affairs, whether it be language, history, race or pure accident. The important thing is that it is there, and that although continually subject to change it has been a dominant feature of the world situation at most time in history – in the Western World particularly since the break up of the feudal system. Moreover, unless we are philosophical anarchists and believe that there are no functions which, for their proper discharge, need the backing of coercive authority, we must admit that some at least of such activities are necessary and in any sane society would have to be done somehow.

Now these independent political entities do not live for themselves. They do not each cultivate their own gardens and leave it at that. Throughout the history of the Western World, there has seldom been a period, save at some time in the age of the Antonines, when there has not been war somewhere. Sometimes this has been pure predation on the part of chiefs and rulers or defence against such activities, sometimes more sophistical claims to tribute or territory; sometimes it has been for religious reasons (genuine or bogus), sometimes for considerations of trade and investment. All this is well known; and although there is much interest in investigating both the ultimate causes of such conflicts – to what extent they have been due to ideology, to what extent to economic causes – and also the way in which economic life has been directly affected by war or the possibility of war as a permanent fact of the situation, that is not the problem of international relations to which I wish to draw attention at this stage.

The problem that we are concerned with here arises from the fact that the direct relations between states as such are not the only relations in the international scene. Subject to the limitations of law and policy, there exist between individuals and groups of individuals in different areas, relationships of a more purely economic nature. They trade one with another; they change their moneys one with another, they make investments in each other's territories. Apart, therefore, from the plane of international political relations as such, there is a plane of individual and group activities cutting right across state divisions and indeed, in the absence of direct intervention by the national states, possessing a far more complex – and more civilised – integration of economic relationships than anything which happens in the purely political area.

Between the two planes, however, there is interaction. Individuals or groups of individuals persuade states to interfere with the market so as to give them privilege and pecuniary advantage. The authorities of the different states, either seeking their personal advantage in cash or power or genuinely concerned to improve the position of their citizens, impose forms of market development which otherwise would not have emerged – tolls, tariffs, prohibition, and so on. Furthermore, as controllers of finance, both of revenue and expenditure and of the supply of money, their policy necessarily influences, either positively or negatively, the *tempo* of economic activity as a whole and therefore the relations between the different systems.

It is the possibility of such interactions which is the focus of attention of political economy in the sphere of international economic relations. As we shall see, considerations of such problems lead inevitably – although this has not always been recognised – to considerations of a wider character, considerations of the political relations between sovereign states and the possibilities of their transformation. But, at the outset, let us concentrate on the more specifically economic problems.

THE CLASSICAL POSITION

Put briefly, the recommendation of Classical Political Economy in this respect was that, as far as possible, the various states should abstain from direct interference with international trade or finance. I hope that I do not have to insist again that this did not mean that they denied to the national states important economic functions in other spheres – the reproach that they preached *laissez-faire* all round is not valid and it becomes a bore to have to say so. It would be valid, however, to say that they recommended that, subject to certain exceptions which I will mention in a moment, the transactions between traders and financiers in different countries, while subject of course to the general rules of law in their respective areas, should be as free as similar transactions within their own borders and as free from financial disturbance. Thus there would be more justification here than elsewhere for the use of the *laissez-faire* label – although its use is usually to be deplored.

Let us examine the grounds for this attitude. As regards trade, with what would then have been regarded as very minor exceptions, the prescription of the Classical system in regard to international transactions was freedom.

This flowed first from a general recognition of mutual advantage in exchange, as opposed to the earlier view that what one man gained another necessarily lost. This was reinforced by an appreciation of the benefits flowing from division of labour not only *within* national areas but also *between* them – the territorial division of labour, as Torrens called it. At first this was propounded in simple common-sense terms of absolute advantages and disadvantages – as witness Adam Smith's celebrated example of the absurdity of growing grapes in Scotland. But eventually this was sharpened up by the *Theory of Comparative Costs* which showed the advantages of trade between areas, differing in absolute cost advantage all round but differing in various degrees. If, for example, West Germany was superior to the United Kingdom both in wine production and woollens but more superior in wine it would be yet advantageous to concentrate on wine and obtain woollens by way of trade. This analysis must surely be regarded as one of the main triumphs of abstract economic thought, far transcending in importance the problems of international trade to which it was first applied; it ultimately explains, not only the advantages arising here, but also any advantages arising from specialisation anywhere where there are unequal differences of potentialities. It establishes, too, principles of action, not only for market economies, but also for any economic organisation which aspires to rational allocation of resources. Other things being equal, a purely Collectivist economy should organise its resources so as to minimise the comparative opportunity costs of achieving any particular goal.

The theory of comparative costs was first developed in 'real' terms involving direct barter transactions. But, as is well known, it was further elaborated so as to show how changes in the distribution of a uniform money stock would bring about price and income relationships conducive to the resource allocation indicated by the 'real' analysis. This was essentially a development of Hume's famous explanation of the self-equilibrating mechanism of the balance of payments in conditions in which there were no independent manufacturers of credit. If the money costs in one area were all below the costs of corresponding products in other areas, then there would be a condition *pro tem* in which the former exported all the products concerned and the latter paid exclusively in specie. But, in the absence of intervention or universal hoarding in the low-cost area, this would lead to a relative rise of prices and incomes there and the reverse process in the area losing specie; so that eventually there would arise a situation in which specie ceased to be transferred and the pattern of trade would assume the relationship which it would have had under conditions of barter. This was Ricardo's famous *Theory of the Distribution of the Precious Metals* well popularised in Senior's *Lectures on the Cost of Obtaining Money* and later modernised and elaborated further in Taussig's celebrated articles on 'Money and Prices in International Trade'.*

As we noted at an earlier stage,† the Classical tradition, at least in its later phases, was not unwilling to admit the possibility of a case for the fostering of infant industries in under-developed countries; and, of course, it always conceded that considerations of defence might dictate the overriding of economic freedom. But, broadly speaking, it would be true to say that the theoretical propositions to which I have just referred constituted a strong presumption of the advantage of trade *between* national areas being ultimately on all fours with the advantages of trade within national areas.

How is the balance kept in the provinces of every kingdom among themselves [asked Hume] but by the force of this principle, which makes it impossible for money to lose its level, and either to rise or sink beyond the proportion of the

---

Quarterly Journal of Economics, xx (1906) pp. 497–522. There is a most beautiful geometrical marriage of the central proposition of the theory of comparative costs and the assumed specie-flow mechanism in Barone's *Principi di Economia Politica* (Rome, 1925) pp. 94–101. It is, of course, not difficult to show how, with independent paper systems approximately managed – an extremely remote possibility – similar results could be obtained by variations in exchange rates.

†See above, p. 40.

labour and commodities which are in each province? Did not long experience make people easy on this head, what a fund of gloomy reflections might calculations afford to a melancholy YORKSHIREMAN, while he computed and magnified the sums drawn to LONDON by taxes, absentees, commodities, and found on comparison the opposite articles so much inferior? And no doubt, had the *Heptarchy* subsisted in ENGLAND, the legislature of each state had been continually alarmed by the fear of a wrong balance; and as it is probable that the mutual hatred of these states would have been extremely violent on account of their close neighbourhood, they would have loaded and oppressed all commerce, by a jealous and superfluous caution.*

A CRITIQUE OF CLASSICISM

Such, in inordinately brief outline, were the prescriptions regarding international economic relations of the famous Classical Political Economy; and a man would indeed be dull of soul who did not admire at once the ingenuity of the arguments and the spacious generosity of the outlook inspiring them. The theory of comparative costs, the idea of self-equilibrating monetary transactions, and the objective of a spontaneous international order, characterised by the mutual benefits of peaceful exchange and territorial division of labour – you must seek long in the history of ideas to find anything so humane and so intellectually well-articulated.

Unfortunately it involved an assumption that no event in previous history had made at all plausible: namely the assumption that, *left to themselves*, the various national authorities would spontaneously abstain from interference. It is doubtful if Adam Smith entertained such an idea. 'To expect . . . that freedom of trade should ever be entirely restored in Great Britain', he said, was 'as absurd as to expect that an Oceana or Utopia should ever be established in it'.†But later writers in the Liberal tradition at least tended to argue as if they did; and this was very odd. For the creation of free trade and common currencies *within* the national areas of the

---

Essays, Moral Political and Literary, ed. Green and Grose, vol. I, pp. 334–5.
†*Wealth of Nations*, vol. I, p. 435.

eighteenth and nineteenth centuries was not the result of a spontaneous demobilisation of obstacles and unification of monetary systems by the cities and principalities and other authorities concerned. The creation of liberal conditions within states had needed the action of central authorities, in the last analysis with the power to coerce, taking away the right to levy local tolls etc. and the power of independent money creation. Looking back ruefully on the frustrated hopes of Classical Liberalism, one may well ask why the exponents thereof should ever have expected of independent national states the self-denying ordinance which they would have never dreamt of expecting from local-government authorities. Certainly if we think of the circumstances of our own time there are no grounds for this kind of optimism.

Money and Credit

This deserves further development. Let me begin therefore by taking up the analysis of the conditions requisite for international monetary equilibrium at the point at which we have just left them in our outline of the general Classical position.

It is the most obvious implication of this position that, in order that there should be equilibrium at fixed exchange rates, it is necessary that local expenditures should vary in relation to each other as they would if in fact there were one general currency rather than many. That is to say that if the payments into an area exceed the payments out, there must be relative expansion there and relative contraction in the reverse position. In this way money changing is just a technical operation and the seamless robe of international payments is maintained.

To illustrate this let us take first a limiting case which is useful by way of contrast. If the internal circulation were to consist wholly of coins minted from the basic metal, and if whatever credit instruments were in circulation were covered by metal to the extent of 100 per cent, and if a similar state of affairs prevailed elsewhere, then the process of adaptation would be a more or less automatic matter. If the balance of payments between one currency area and the rest were not in equilibrium, then there would be shifts in the distribution of metal, which operating on prices, incomes and employment in the areas concerned would tend to bring about a new equilibrium. The fact that the moneys in the different areas were expressed in different units would be a trivial matter: to all intents and purposes the circulations in the different areas would behave as if there were one money. There would be no guarantee of the absolute value of the moneys in such a system; but their relations to various commodity groups would be the same when reduced to a common weight. This is the theory of the specie-flow mechanism immortalised in Hume's famous essay *On the Balance of Trade*.

Once, however, we make the more realistic assumption that there are means of exchange supplementary to, or replacing, a purely metallic money, possibilities of disharmony emerge. If in the different national areas there are facilities for the independent creation of credit in the shape of notes, then clearly there is no guarantee that the relationships of the different monetary systems will necessarily move harmoniously so as to preclude, or at least rapidly to eliminate, disequilibria in balances of payments. And historical experience shows that the possibility of such disharmony is very real. It is worth noting that this was clearly perceived and stated by Hume himself, the author of the standard specie-flow analysis from which so much of the Classical position in respect of inter- national policy derived. 'I scarcely know', he argued, in the famous essay, *On the Balance of Trade* already quoted, 'any method of sinking money below its level, but these institutions of banks, funds, and paper credit, which are so much practised, in this Kingdom. These render paper equivalent to money, make it supply the place of gold and silver, circulate it through- out the whole state, raise proportionately the price of labour and commodities, and by that means either banish a great part of those precious metals or prevent their increase.'*

Now, of course, this is not to say that once credit arrange- ments are in existence the equilibration of international balances of payments is impossible. If the various banking systems so arrange their policies that inward surpluses involve relative expansion and outward deficits relative contraction – please note the word *relative* in this connection – so that the

Essays, Moral Political and Literary, p. 337.

combined aggregate expenditures still conform to what would happen under a common money, all will still be well. There was division among the Classical Economists concerning the means of securing this harmony. All agreed that it must rest upon a basis of convertibility of credit instruments into the precious metals concerned. But, as we have seen already, one school of thought, the Currency School, argued that this obligation must be reinforced by compulsory obligations as regards backing for the note issue: the other, the Banking School, opposed the singling out of the note issue for obligations as regards special cover and urged chiefly the combination of interest policy with greatly increased reserves. In practice neither prescription worked. The compulsory cover for notes was enacted but the omission of any requirement as regards other forms of credit meant that financial crises still occurred. The recommendation of higher reserves was never followed, so that any damaging deficits on the overseas account were left to be dealt with at much shorter notice and with greater severity than would have been the case had there been this much greater elbow-room. Nevertheless, in one way or another, with occasional periods of anxiety and some breakdowns in some areas, the system worked up to the general breakdown of 1914–18.

It is worth noting further that the ardours and endurances of such a system can be greatly exaggerated. Careless use of the terms 'inflation' or 'deflation' which, strictly speaking, should apply only to aggregates – whether a closed system or a world of systems linked together by observance of common rules – has invested the idea of the relative movements within such systems with undue terrors. If, other things being equal, the demand for, say, canned beer increases, we should not normally describe the increase of receipts and perhaps prices of the brewers as *inflation*, any more than we should describe a movement away from, say, soft drinks, as *deflation*. Similar inhibitions should apply to the discussion of shifts within the aggregate of international expenditure in such terms – an increase of money incomes in a national area due to a greater real demand for its products as inflation, or a corresponding decrease elsewhere as deflation – especially since, in a generally advancing world system, such changes are *relative* rather than *absolute.* In a world in which total money supply is increasing at a rate commensurate with productivity in general, an unfavourable balance of payments for one area does not necessarily involve an absolute contraction of aggregate expenditure there, but only a slowing down of increase relative to the areas enjoying favourable balances. An absolute contraction is not excluded. But it is by no means inevitable.

Nevertheless, it is all too clear that, with governments and central banks entertaining different conceptions of appropriate internal policy and offsetting deficits by new creations of credit or surpluses by abnormal hoarding, there may easily arise strains and stresses within the system of international payments which lead to exchange crises and the rupture of any system of fixed parities. A central bank, committed to a policy of cheap money, in circumstances in which the fundamental market situation would call for higher rates, may well set up movements adverse to a satisfactory balance of payments. A government intent on a policy of full employment, whatever the movement of incomes in relation to the value of the product, will almost certainly run into similar difficulties, unless other governments are inspired by the same sentiments to expansions of expenditure in the same proportion.

The assumption therefore on which the Classical argument in respect of international monetary equilibrium was too often implicitly based, namely that completely independent sovereign states can be relied upon to manage their financial policies so that disequilibrium at fixed parities is unlikely to arise, was based upon too optimistic an estimate of how governments usually behave.

It is sometimes thought – indeed the idea is very fashionable in quarters of the highest professional competence – that the central Classical assumption of automatic equilibration of balances of payments and territorial division of labour according to the principles of comparative cost and reciprocal demand can be maintained if the attempt to maintain fixed parities is abandoned and exchange rates are allowed to fluctuate completely freely. The idea is not unattractive superficially; and much ingenious argument has been devoted to its recommendation. Models can certainly be constructed in which movements of the exchange rate, other things being equal, perform the same allocative function between the different national areas as do gold movements in the models in the Ricardian mode of simple specie-flow relationships. But with the best will in the world to find a simple way out of the complications of contemporary international monetary problems, I cannot persuade myself that such proposals do justice, either to the complexities of the world with which current financial policy has to deal or indeed to the ultimate presuppositions of the Liberal ideal.

In order to avoid misunderstanding, let me at once make clear what my eventual strictures do *not* imply.

First they do *not* imply that a single rate, floating in a world in which the remaining areas are maintaining more or less fixed parities, is either inexpedient or disastrous. If the area in question has got badly out of equilibrium, and there is doubt concerning what parity would be appropriate, there is a strong case for a period of experimental floating. Nor can it be argued that it is necessarily a disaster if one small area or even a large consolidated bloc adopted such a policy for a longer period, provided – which, as we shall see, is a doubtful assumption – that its internal policy is not such as to create external disequilibrium. The reservations which I wish to ventilate apply to free floating rates all round for the different monetary systems of the world as a permanent system and as a system which conforms to the basic Liberal ideals.

Let us begin with practical realities. There has never been such a system and in all probability there never will be. The jargon of the theory makes a distinction between 'free' floating and 'dirty' floating, the one being literally what it says, the other being floating subject to all sorts of interventions and controls. Now 'dirty' floating is something which we know very well: anyone who has had to purchase foreign exchange for transitory visits abroad, still more than anyone who has wished to move capital from one area to another, has come into contact with the actual apparatus prevailing in present circumstances in most countries of the world. But free floating, in the sense of abstention from all this and no intervention on the part of central banks, either to support a local currency for political reasons or to defeat the alleged machinations of speculators, has never been a frequent spectacle; and that it should be generalised in a world either of dictatorships or democracies is very difficult to imagine.

Moreover, abstracting from all this, with all the evasions and complications to which it gives rise, we should also note, as an accompaniment of floating exchanges, their probable indirect effects on internal policies. To maintain internal stability of the local purchasing power of money is an operation requiring great prudence and circumspection, even if it operates under the constraints of an implicit obligation to maintain something like a fixed parity. If this constraint is abandoned and the rate is free, then, politics apart, the business of preventing the floating rate giving rise to internal complications, uncompensated rises with prices of imports, claims for increased incomes to offset changes in the cost of living caused by downward movements in the exchange rate and so on, is not easy to handle even in a polity of angels. Given the actual quality of those who rule over most free countries at present, the probability is that the assumption will be, as with a recent government in the United Kingdom, that the rate of exchange will 'look after' the balance of payments and that, therefore, an internal policy of deficit financing may be conducted without the necessity of considering its external repercussions.

Let us ignore these mundane considerations and consider a little the pure theory of the subject. The obvious case for it is the greater ease with which, in the absence of countervailing movements, changes in the international conditions of demand and supply can be made to influence the real incomes of the individuals in the areas concerned by changes in exchange rates rather than by changes in money incomes and the prices of internally produced goods. Assuming the existence of what has come to be called 'money illusion' – the state of affairs in which incentives in the labour market and elsewhere are governed principally by a fixed focus on the number of monetary units received rather than considerations of what they will purchase – this would be so: a change in exchange rates cheapening exports and making imports dearer is likely to be accompanied, initially at least, by less friction than changes in internal money incomes and costs. The academic advocates of floating rates have usually reached their position by way of pessimism regarding the working of individual markets in this respect. Few of them perhaps realise how much their hopes of evading these difficulties depend on the width of the area affected by the rate of exchange: if there were different rates of exchange for each area producing *single* groups of commodities, any absence of perception of the difference between prices in the local money and their equivalence in foreign exchange could hardly evade notice.

But even assuming sufficiently large areas diversified sufficiently for the connection between prices and incomes expressed in one money and in others to escape immediate notice, it is really not at all plausible to assume that *nobody* except the dealers in exchange markets will notice it. And once this process begins, then, *in the absence of controls*, there will be a growing tendency *to make contracts in terms of the currency in respect of which expectations are most favourable* – to lose value least or to gain it most. This is not a figment of the imagination. It is just what happened in regard to dealings in gold and silver when there were parallel currencies in such media in earlier days. It is just what happened in Western Europe in the depreciation of the 1920s ere the techniques of exchange control had been perfected: in Germany and other areas affected with monetary instability more and more contracts were made in terms of sterling – then a strong currency – and dollars. In free conditions, that is to say the use of the weaker moneys would shrink; in contrast to the *centrifugal* tendencies created by independent national policies in regard to the divergence of monetary standards, the *centripetal* forces of self-interest would tend to the unification of dealings in the money anticipated to be strongest.

This then is the logical outcome of the so-called 'liberal' solution to the international monetary problem, namely without a deliberate prohibition of the tendency to make contracts in incomes other than one's own, the system would not be viable. The maintenance of free floating exchanges involves, as did Plato's money in the odious Totalitarian Community of the *Laws*,* ferocious sanctions against dealings in any but the money of the local state. It is surely an ironical circumstance that some of the advocates of this system are true liberals, yet this supreme limitation on the economic freedom of the individual seems to leave them unperturbed.

* *The Dialogues of Plato*, trans. Benjamin Jowett (1875) vol. v, pp. 313–14.

Trade

We may now turn to the Classical prescriptions in regard to trade and commercial policy.

It must be clear first that these prescriptions and the expectations founded thereon were based on a gross under-estimate of the strength of producer interest in shaping the economic policies of governments. The noble and idealistic minds who were responsible for this school of thought actually believed that, once their analysis had been released to the world, the obvious interest of consumers would sweep aside any resistance by groups of producers. Adam Smith and his friends were under no such delusion. They knew, to quote his words, that 'people of the same trade seldom meet together, even for merriment and diversion but the conversation ends in a conspiracy against the public, or in some contrivance to raise prices'. But many nineteenth-century Liberals were less down to earth. They ignored the fact that the group interest of producers is much more direct and continuous than that of the general body of consumers, and tends to much greater solidarity and readiness for concerted action. Their hopes, therefore, for abstention of democracies from policies inimical to consumer interest were vastly exaggerated, as history, alas, has shown.

Beyond this they certainly under-estimated the real difficulties involved in passing from the policy of protection, in which most of the states were involved, to the state of free trade which they recommended. In the contemplation of the ultimately beneficial effects of unilateral demobilisation of obstruction, they tended to overlook the possibilities of adverse consequences in the transition *via* changes in the terms of trade. They were not at all unaware of the theoretical possibility of forms of restrictionism which, by exploiting monopolistic positions, might bring local advantage, though, rightly in my judgement, they tended to dismiss these as unlikely to be often realised in practice. But, with the exception of Robert Torrens, they certainly did not appreciate sufficiently that the short-run effects of removal of restrictions might have adverse effects, not merely on the protected industries but also on the foreign-trade position of the area as a whole.*

*The long-run pros and cons of the so-called 'terms of trade' argument for

If we add to this the pretext for fairly arbitrary and indiscriminate tariffs afforded by the perfectly valid argument for
the protection of infant industries, not to mention the much
more doubtful extension of such measures to what I have called
'invalid' industries, so politically rewarding with unsophisti-
cated or interested political electorates, you have a climate of
opinion which makes highly improbable the achievement of the
Liberal hope that realisation of long-run national interest would
lead to a general abstention from interference with international trade. The brief period in the nineteenth century when,
following the demobilisation of British protectionism and the
repeal of the Corn Laws, the movement to free trade had some
popularity, can be seen in retrospect to have been, at least as
much an historical fluke as the result of widespread understanding. 'It was dammed potatoes that did it', said the Duke
of Wellington of the Corn Law episode; and although, like
almost all short propositions about social movements, this was a
very considerable over-simplification, it was perhaps as near the
truth as the view which regarded it just as a triumph for the
sweet reason and persuasiveness of the few people who really
understood the valid, as distinct from the popular, arguments
for free trade.

Thus, from what I have said, both in regard to trade and to
money and credit, it should be clear that the wider hopes
built on Classical analyses were based on delusion. To expect
that, once their interest had been sufficiently understood and
promulgated, the policies of independent states would be
conducted as to leave international trade and payments
much as they would have been in a world in which there was
one co-ordinating authority had small justification in common
sense or common experience. Expectations based on such
assumptions prove in this respect to have little more practical
foundation than the windy generalisations of Godwinian
philosophical anarchism. The absence of a common framework
of law and order for the organisations called sovereign states
leaves international economic relations in chaos, alas with all

import and export duties is nowhere better discussed than Marshall's 'Memoran-
dum on the Fiscal Policy of International Trade', Marshall: *Official Papers* (1926)
pp. 36-42. But in my judgement he under-estimated the short-run difficulties of
unilateral dismantlement.

the danger to international political relations and international peace that that may so easily involve.

What then remains?

At any rate there is still an ideal. If the Classical hopes proved wrong, the model on which they built their analysis is still attractive in this respect. At least it is for me. The idea that the exchange of goods and services between individuals in different national areas should be as free as similar exchanges within those areas still seems to me to be one of the desiderata of a sensibly organised world. So too does the idea of monetary arrangements which function as if there were one money. It may be that, for some younger people, the current state of affairs with its exchange controls, its arbitrary regulation of the export of capital, its blatant bribery of the electorates of particular industries and its complete uncertainties are part of the order of nature. But for me, I confess, they are a sign and a symbol of much that is divisive in human society – a state of affairs which we should try to surpass.

But how to do this, that is the question. A world federation with commercial and monetary regulations as federal functions is obviously out of the question, at any rate in our lifetime. Having regard to the differences of ultimate ideology, not to mention stages of development and demographic tendencies, many people, even of Liberal tendencies, would positively fight against it. The more you think about it, the more practical difficulties present themselves. We shall need to review very thoroughly our ideas of constitutional structure and representation before we get near a workable conception of a federation of the world.

In our time the most favoured alternatives have been looser collective arrangements between states sufficiently like-minded to enter into anything beyond *ad hoc* bilateral treaties: in the sphere of trade, periodic meetings under the auspices of GATT to agree generally applicable relaxation of commercial restrictions negotiated bilaterally but taking place at the same time and spreading their benefits by way of most-favoured-nation clauses. And in the sphere of money, loose agreements regarding rules of procedure for changing rates of exchange and some pooling of resources for mutual aid as attempted in the statutes of the International Monetary Fund – the

Bretton Woods system, perhaps revised and reformulated.

Unfortunately such expedients do not carry us very far. Commercial agreements can be revoked or circumnavigated and, while the power of independent credit manipulation persists, the best-laid schemes of international monetary order are apt to come to grief as we have seen in recent years. We should not under-estimate what has been done in the years since the Second World War to clear the channels of international trade and finance. But we deceive ourselves if we believe that what remains goes far to guarantee continuity of order even in those countries of the free world where there is a will to progress in this connection. In the last analysis nothing which stops short of the taking over from such national states as are willing powers of initiative in regard to the regulation of trade and money, as, in the past, the national states have taken over such functions from townships and other local authorities, can achieve the Classical ideal.

Clearly this raises wider issues which are better discussed in the overtly political context which is the subject of my concluding chapter.

INTERNATIONAL ECONOMIC RELATIONS UNDER COLLECTIVISM

Before proceeding thus, however, it is worthwhile investigating international relations under Collectivism. This is not an 'academic' digression, using 'academic' in the vulgar politician's sense of the word – any thought which looks beyond the week after next. Substantial areas of the world are now under Total Collectivist regimes. We are not speculating in the void.

Now it is not impossible to conceive of a world of Collectivist states in which the allocation of resources and the resulting pattern of trade conformed approximately to the Classical ideal. If the various sovereign authorities planned their economies according to the general principles of opportunity costs, devoting their labour and material resources to those branches of activity in which their comparative advantages were greatest, leaving the rest of their consumption to be obtained by way of exchange, this would be so: and if a world

Collectivist authority were in control and – which we have seen to be most improbable – it were in a position to calculate costs and effective demand, then it might be hoped that, exercising a degree of regard for personal liberty in choice, which would be most unlikely in an apparatus of administration enjoying such unprecedented and terrifying power – such a pattern might conceivably emerge.

But in a world of separate Collectivist authorities such an emergence would be highly improbable. For, in such a situation, if they followed the Classical precepts, the plans of each authority would be subject to a multitude of changes *outside their jurisdiction*. They would have to be adapted to external as well as internal conditions – and this would seem to be a sacrifice of that unity of control which it is said to be the main purpose of Collectivism to achieve. Thus, although the facts of life being what they are, it would not be possible altogether to eliminate economic relations with other states, there would be at least a tendency to try to achieve as much self-sufficiency as possible: and what commerce took place with the rest of the world would take the form of bulk-dealing, long-term contracts, bilateral bargaining and so on in which tendencies to conform to the pattern of trade based on considerations of comparative costs would play a very small part. So we reach the interesting insight that while International Collectivism, if free from the political and economic disadvantages examined in an earlier chapter, might tend to preserve the international division of labour, National Collectivism would tend to destroy it. Such speculative considerations are not out of harmony with the state of the world as we know it.

But in fact the position is worse than this. The desire for self-sufficiency may involve sacrifices which would be diminished if the area of jurisdiction were greater; and since under Collectivism the distinction between property and territory tends to fade, there would be powerful tendencies to expansionary domination on the part of Collectivist powers whose authorities had, or thought they had, superior military potential. If one assumes a world whose constituent states, apart from the maintenance of law and order and the provision of services deemed essential, refrained from direction of the organisation of production, in such circumstances the area of the state jurisdiction would be a matter of secondary importance, apart from considerations of defence. When the thirteen American colonies at first became independent it was not an inhibiting circumstance to the growth of the British textile industry. But under Collectivism it is different. The extent of territory may affect materially the management of the plan. No doubt there are ideological grounds for the tight control of Eastern European countries by the power of Soviet Russia. But the increased scope for what is ironically called 'co-operation' is not a negligible factor.

It was the ambition of the Classical Economists that freedom of commercial intercourse would diminish the danger of international conflict. The considerations advanced in this section constitute a legitimate fear that a world of National Collectivism would be more, rather than less, liable to international conflict arising from economic causes.*

LAISSEZ-PASSER

There is one further matter, arising particularly in the field of international economic relations, which deserves brief notice – the problems of the migrations of people.

The maxim *laissez-faire* has been coupled historically with the maxim *laissez-passer* although their origins were different.†
But in the eighteenth-century setting it applied principally to the restriction on movements within states which were then prevalent. As I have mentioned already, Adam Smith devoted considerable space to strictures on the law of settlement which imposed severe limitations on movement between parishes. Later on, when migration on an international scale became conspicuous, the ideal of *laissez-passer* seems to have passed insensibly into the general ideology of persons of liberal habits of thought. I well remember, at a tender age, asking my mother the meaning of the word passport. 'Oh that', she replied, 'is something which you have to have in Russia where the people are unhappy.'

*In this connection perhaps I might be permitted to refer to my *Economic Causes of War* (1940, reprinted New York, 1968) where the questions here touched upon briefly were discussed at much greater length.

†For a detailed historical exegesis see August Oncken, *Die Maxime Laissez Faire et Laissez Passer* (Bern, 1886).

Now there can be no doubt that, *in a world of constant or uniformly increasing population* – please note the qualification – the absence of barriers to movement would tend to the advantage of productive efficiency. There would be a tendency for movement from areas and industries where productivity at the margin was relatively smaller than it was elsewhere, to areas and industries where it was greater. I know of no analysis, however sophisticated, which would deny that, in such circumstances, production in general measured in price terms would tend to be greater than in a similar world in which barriers to movement persisted.

Furthermore, if we move to the more exalted plane of social ethics the general argument for *laissez-passer* is no less convincing. Freedom of movement is both a sign and a symbol of a civilised society. No doubt it will often be resisted by interested groups whose monopolistic positions may be thereby threatened – the usual motive for public opposition. It may also be prohibited by totalitarian governments who do not wish their subjects to see for themselves the fruits of freedom elsewhere. In Voltaire's *History of Charles XII*, it is related how, in eighteenth-century Russia, freedom to travel abroad was withheld from the citizens save by permission of the authorities, a 'law', adds Voltaire, 'avowedly enacted to prevent them from realising their state of bondage'.* Neither in that day nor in this can such grounds for restriction be regarded by persons of moral sensibility with anything but extreme repulsion. The barbed wire (and the graves of would-be escapers) of the Berlin Wall are emblems of an ultimate obscenity.

Unfortunately in a world of easy communication, diverse languages and customs and unequal rates of population increase, there are certain arguments against *laissez-passer* which are not ethically despicable. If, in an area claiming independent sovereignty, there occurs a sudden incursion of large numbers speaking a different language and with markedly different social customs, there may rise such intense reaction among the local inhabitants, that, in the interests of civil order, there may be a case for some limitation of the rate of entry. There are all sorts of ethical reasons which can be adduced against such a policy – not to mention the fact that too often

---

*History of Charles XII, trans. Todhunter (Everyman edn, 1908) p.22.

when it is contemplated, it is urged by the ignorant or the politically interested. But it is difficult to deny that occasions might arise when, on purely dispassionate grounds, it could be defended as a lesser evil. In my youth it used to be said 'let the common people of the world intermix and there will be no international conflict'. Alas, we now know that this is not so and that in fact it needs a high degree of educated sophistication to move easily among people of different languages and different habits.

There is, moreover, in the present condition of the world, a much less disputable case for some suspension of *laissez-passer*, namely that which rests upon the tendencies in certain areas to indefinite increases of population. If it be admitted that extreme over-population is an evil and if it be the case that, in certain areas, there prevail tendencies to such a condition, then I see no resisting the argument that there is no moral obligation for the inhabitants or parts where such tendencies do not exist or are in process of elimination to acquiesce in the spread of excessive increase to their own areas. Indeed on the most severe grounds of general utility there is every reason against it. There is no obligation to let what has yet emerged of reasonably high standards and culture for all be submerged by uncontrolled animal reproduction. As Edwin Cannan, the most cosmopolitan idealist among economists of the Classical tradition, argued, 'If any people acts as if its ideal of progress was, in J. S. Mill's picturesque phrase, "a human anthill" it is probably desirable that it should be confined within as narrow limits as possible. It is better that it should learn that over-population is an evil and how to avoid it, in one country or continent than after extending it all over the world.'*

It may be that in times to come the cogency of this conclusion will be rendered irrelevant by a sufficient spread of rational habits in regard to multiplication – in which case limitation of free movement could only be defended on the grounds of mitigating the reaction to ignorant prejudice. But, in the present state of affairs, in certain parts of the world, and having regard to the intractable nature of the habits and ideology of their inhabitants, it is to be feared that we have to live with conditions which render the pure theory of *laissez-passer*

* *Wealth of Nations*, 3rd edn (1928) p. 287.

inapplicable. We may assume that the influences tending to stationary population in other parts – for example Western Europe and North America – are such as to allow risks to be taken in the formation of areas of free movement; nothing that I have said in this connection should be held to vindicate obstacles to free movement through the Western World as a whole – I should certainly be prepared to assume there at least the eventual spread of family limitation, even among the adherents of creeds which at present condemn it. But elsewhere it is simply digging our heads in the sands to ignore the very real dangers of present tendencies.*

---

*Recognition of these dangers should not be held to vindicate limitation on the movement of all persons from such areas. But it does justify quite severe educational tests.

CHAPTER 11
Politics and Political Economy

INTRODUCTION

The programme proposed at the end of the first chapter is now almost completed. I have attempted an appraisal in broad outline of the prescriptions of Classical Political Economy in the main fields with which it was concerned: consumption, the organisation of production, the stability of the system as a whole, welfare and distribution and international trade; and I have digressed to compare those aspects of Collectivism which are not in conflict with the fundamental Classical prescriptions and those which obviously are. But, save incidentally, I have not yet examined the broader political assumptions which inspired the Classical writers and discussed them in the light of experience and thought since that day. That is the object of this concluding chapter.

THE SYSTEM OF ECONOMIC FREEDOM AND ITS ULTIMATE JUSTIFICATION

As we have seen, the essence of the Classical outlook was an insistence on the liberty of individuals and groups of individuals when that liberty did not infringe the liberty of others. As we have also seen, that insistence inevitably assumed an apparatus of law and order and it involved also positive coercive and collective action when the functions involved were unlikely to be performed by individuals or groups of individuals. There will be more to be said about that later. But at this stage the centre of gravity of our enquiry is the rationale of the insistence on liberty.

Now I do not think that this is to be explained merely in

H

terms of the belief that the system works and can work tolerably well if it is allowed to do so. It is quite true that the demonstration of the extent of the division of labour guided by the impersonal mechanisms of the market which was the main theme of the central analysis of the *Wealth of Nations* is to be regarded as a leading feature of the Classical outlook. And, indeed, the unveiling of the potentialities of an organisation of production, not imposed from above but arising spontaneously from individual or group initiative within a framework of law and order, is undoubtedly one of the great sociological discoveries of all time. It has continued its influence from that age to this and has been sharpened further more recently by the detailed analysis of demand developed by the not altogether appropriately named 'utility theories'. It would certainly be quite misleading to deny that the conception of the self-regulating mechanism of markets, and the scope of decentralised initiative that it involved, contributed much to the praise of liberty to be found in the Classical writings and to later work following the same tradition.

It would be a mistake, however, to regard it as the ultimate justification. Adam Smith's 'Natural Liberty' was extolled because it worked. But it worked to satisfy preferences as expressed in effective demand; and the preferences were preferences uninhibited by authority, save in so far as they infringed the preferences of others. The approbation of the mechanism was not an approbation of the mechanism as an end; it was essentially approbation of a means, a means permitting the maximum of liberty in the expression of individual choice and adaptation to the environment.

But why then this emphasis on liberty? The majority of the Classical writers who, with the possible exception of Adam Smith,* in one sense or other, can be described as Utilitarians, would have argued that, since the ultimate objective was the maximisation of happiness and since the individual was better capable of judging for himself than any authority, a state of liberty was essential for the satisfaction of this criterion. Today,

---

*The qualification is inserted to show that I am not unaware of the strictures which have been passed by Professor Macfie (see his *Individual in Society: Papers on Adam Smith*, 1967) and others on his inclusion in this broad classification. But it is an olive branch rather than a confession of guilt.

provided that, following Karl Popper, we reformulate this aim as the minimisation of pain – which has the advantage of lending less countenance to authoritarian versions – there is still much to be said for this contention. Even John Stuart Mill, whose *On Liberty* must forever remain one of the classical statements of the philosophy of the subject, was apt to state his case in terms of the benefits resulting from free initiative and free enquiry; and, however much we may wish to add to it, who would wish to subtract from the weight of his argument?

Nevertheless I personally doubt whether this way of putting things goes completely to the heart of the matter. We may agree that the free adult educated citizen is probably better able to choose for himself enjoyments and activities which increase his happiness or diminish his pain than persons who may have coercive powers over him – though we must admit that, in the end, this is an empirical judgement. But we must agree too that, regarded in this way, liberty is a means rather than an end and that unquestionably it can have effects which we should regard as bad as well as those which we should regard as good. There is nothing in the nature of the world which obliges us to believe that liberty of the individual or groups of individuals *necessarily* leads to actions which on any ethical criterion are good.

In spite of this, however, I think we can assert that it is *only* actions which are free which are eligible for that description in that context. We may describe a drought as bad and an abundant harvest as good; but there is no ethical implication in such language unless we regard these events as expressing the will of the President of the Universe – which not everybody would be willing to do. The same is true of human conduct. Action which is imposed from above may have *consequences* which, in some sense or other, are either good or bad. But it is only actions which are freely chosen, which *in themselves* qualify for such designation. The rest, together with other events in the physical world – earthquakes or the movements of cattle – are the effects of mere physical causation.

This, surely, is the ultimate case for liberty. Not that it necessarily leads to actions which are good in themselves or that it is a safeguard against actions which are bad in themselves, but rather that it is a *necessary condition* of decisions which can be the subject of any strictly ethical judgement; and that only where it prevails is human action subject to moral categories. I do not claim to know whether this formulation would have had the endorsement of Classical libertarians. But I would submit that it provides their ultimate objectives with a justification of very considerable force.

THE FUNCTIONS OF THE STATE – LIMITATIONS

In preceding chapters I have again and again emphasised how the pursuit of liberty involves an apparatus of law and regulation in order that the liberty of some may not infringe the liberty of others. I have discussed, too, in various connections, the positive functions of the state both in regard to the provision of indiscriminate benefit and in regard to welfare and distribution. But before proceeding to questions of the political constitution of the state thus conceived, it is perhaps desirable to take another glance at the evolution of opinion concerning the area of state operation in general. It might be thought that the answer to such a question flows inevitably from the summation of the answers given to specific problems. But I think that there is more in it than this, and that, in any case, it is worthwhile discussing it explicitly.

It was not the Classical Economists who formulated the maxim that to govern well you must govern little. Its author was a predecessor of the French Physiocrats, the famous Marquis d'Argenson.* But I have no doubt that it would have been treated with respect by the British Classical writers, although, as can be shown, their conceptions of the functions of government considerably transcended those of the French School;† and, as time has gone on, such conceptions have been broadened in many directions. The works of Bentham, who, although not orthodox in the Classical sense in regard to some matters of analysis, especially the theory of money, must be regarded as highly influential in shaping conceptions of appropriate policy, abound with novel ideas concerning extensions of government activity. But he too would not have refused assent to the general principle. Indeed some of the

*See Oncken, *Die Maxime Laissez Faire et Laissez Passer.*
†See my *Theory of Economic Policy*, especially ch. II.

sharpest formulations of the prescriptions are to be found in his writings.* It was Bentham who recalled the saying, attributed to Diogenes, 'stand out of my sunshine', as an injunction to interfering governments.

Why was this? Historically there are two reasons which can be cited. First, it must be remembered that, at the time at which the Classical outlook developed, the machinery of government was both corrupt and inefficient. The reforms which gave to Great Britain a central civil service not open to sinister influence and probably more efficient than most elsewhere had not yet been enacted; and, for this reason, many operations which nowadays we should unhesitatingly expect of government were not within the range of practicability. The influence of some Classical thinkers, especially Bentham and his followers, did indeed contribute to the evolution of greater effectiveness of the machinery of government. But there were still reasons for avoiding the invocation of state action, if the reasons for such recourse were not overwhelmingly compelling.

Much more important than this, however, was the fact that a great many of the things which government actually did at those times were positively antipathetic to the Classical outlook. Many of the regulations and interventions of those days were in spheres where, on the central Classical analysis, regulation and intervention were not only unnecessary but also positively harmful. They involved interference both with freedom of choice on the part of the consumer and with the freedom of initiative on the part of producers; and while, as we have seen, the Classical outlook was prepared to admit certain exceptions for purposes of defence and even for the fostering of infant industries, the general presumption was that the allocation of resources thus produced was inferior to that which, given a proper framework of law and order, would have emerged under freedom. The Classical outlook abhorred paternalism in the ordinary business of life; and paternalism, in its view, involved the intrusion of government into spheres of activity where it was unnecessary.

*It was these formulations that misled Keynes, obviously not widely read in Bentham and Benthamiana, to erect him as a sort of Aunt Sally in his famous, but in this respect, highly misleading, *End of Laissez Faire*. See his *Collected Works*, vol. x, p. 279.

Much as things have changed since then, in my judgement considerations similar to those set forth here are still relevant. As regards the machinery of government, while the technical excellence and integrity of the central public service has doubtless improved very greatly in some parts of the world, it is also true that its efficiency in the discharge of business is still subject to severe limitations. Partly this is due to the extent of what it is asked to undertake: the magnitude of the tasks assigned to the machinery of government in the so-called Mixed State is such as to depress the efficiency of a squadron of archangels let alone the capacity of the talented officials of modern public administration – I fancy that the impartial historian of the future will attribute some at least of our misfortunes since 1935 to the fact that so much of our business has been in the hands of men soaked with fatigue-toxins. Partly it is due to the necessary requirements of democratic government. The most efficient business executives will display the qualities associated with bureaucracy if placed in a position subject to parliamentary question and to the logic which requires action congruous with existing precedent. Much of the best intellect in a community such as the United Kingdom in the present day is concentrated in the administrative grade of the civil service. But if one considers the magnitude of the tasks which the wisdom of Parliament lays upon them, the verdict on much of what they do must be similar to that of Dr Johnson's (wrong-headed) pronouncement on female preaching, that the wonder is, not that it is done well but that it is done at all.

Parallel considerations apply to the substance of policy. It is unfortunately not true that the reproach of paternalism is any less applicable to many of the actions of government in our own day than in the days of the emergence of the Classical system. Needless intervention to limit the scope of individual initiative, both in the sphere of consumption and production, still complicates both the allocation of resources and the efficiency of production. Indeed on a broad view, the degree of this kind of policy is probably even more extensive. If one considers the diversion of resources to foster this or that political objective – agrarian protectionism, the support of obsolescent industry, the fostering of cartels and restrictive practices generally – it is difficult to believe that the mournful catalogue of the deficiencies of the Mercantile System as enumerated by Adam Smith could not be surpassed by the contemporary policies of most modern industrial nations – not to mention the almost comic-opera absurdities of some at least of the so-called under-developed communities.

For both these reasons therefore – considerations of executive efficiency and the undesirability of the intrusion of government into areas of individual or group initiative which would function better without it – without in any way denying the importance of the essential functions of the state and their necessary increase in modern industrial societies, there is still much good sense in the presumption that the state action should be confined to those spheres in which it is doing things which if they are not done by government are not done at all. In the last analysis the famous formula of Maynard Keynes in his *End of Laissez Faire*, already cited, is not a refutation* but rather a reinterpretation of d'Argenson's maxim that to govern well one must govern little.

Such considerations apart, however, there is a deeper justification for this presumption which links up with the rationale of liberty developed in the preceding section. As we have seen at an earlier stage, collective as opposed to individual choice, if it is not unanimous, involves the overruling of some individual preferences. The consumer, bidding in the market, exercises an influence proportionate to his bid. Given the initial distribution of resources, it is an election, so to speak with exactly proportional representation. In contrast to this state of affairs, the voter in any practical system of collective choice has to accept the decision of the majority: in such circumstances, therefore, the wishes of the minority are overruled. This is certainly not an argument against collective decisions as such: on the contrary, where decisions involving indiscriminate benefit are involved, they are inevitable if important functions are not to be left undischarged. But it is certainly an argument for keeping the area of such decisions to the minimum compatible with good sense. Again we should not argue that the state should *never* assume functions which may conceivably be discharged by individual decisions: there are marginal areas, particularly as regards the educational and eleemosynary functions where the penumbra

*Chapter I, p. 9 above.

of the so-called 'neighbourhood effects' may be a matter of reasonable dispute. But we should argue that where individual initiative in consumption and production is practical, there the burden of proof that collective decision is desirable rests very definitely on its advocates: the presumption is the other way. On this very fundamental plan, therefore, for societies, which recognise the ultimate ethical justification of liberty, the presumption remains that to govern well it is desirable to govern little.

LIBERTY AND THE FORM OF GOVERNMENT

Belief in the necessity of coercive authority to create and enforce law and to perform those functions which it is not in the interests of individuals to perform does not in itself determine the way in which such authority should be constituted. Should the ultimate power be vested in one person or many? Should tenure be by birth or by election? If the latter, on what basis should election take place? Must all power be concentrated in one organ or is a division conceivable and practical? Are there fundamental constitutional principles to which detailed laws and administrative acts must conform. These are standard questions which have been the preoccupation of political philosophy through the ages.

Now it is unquestionable that, at certain periods of history, with governments which by no stretch of the imagination can be described as libertarian, there has been extensive freedom of individual action, both as regards production and consumption. The division of labour, governed by the impersonal forces of the market, has not waited for the emergence of democratic regimes in order to develop its powerful potentialities. There have been – and are – authoritarian regimes which have inhibited initiative in production and freedom of choice in consumption. But there have also been other such regimes under which such freedoms have been widespread. Incidentally it is also to be observed that, in some regimes of the present day which may legitimately be described as 'democratic', in the sense of a more or less universal franchise in public elections, such individual liberties are very considerably circumscribed. But our concern at this stage is with government as such and of the fact that non-democratic authority in this sphere has not always been inimical to liberty in other respects. As Professor Hayek has emphasised in his classic *Constitution of Liberty*,* general liberty, in the sense of the absence of constraints on individual activities which do not impinge on the liberties of others, is intellectually separable from political liberty in the sense of the right to vote; and it is clear that, historically, the movement for widening the franchise has by no means always been associated with movements for individual liberty in the former sense.

Nevertheless, if we take the concept of liberty in its widest legitimate connotation as an absence of necessary constraints,† it is surely true that not to be allowed to participate, in some way or other, in making the law under which one has to live, to be prevented if necessary by fine or force from entering the polling booth, must be described as a deprivation of liberty; and that the voteless citizen of mature age and sufficient education, however free in other respects, must be regarded as suffering a discriminatory exclusion. If we have regard to the way in which this has operated in some communities, even in modern times, where women and literate non-whites are concerned, this cannot be regarded as an unimportant limitation.

At the same time it must be recognised that liberty in this respect is to be conceived on a plane different from that of individual choice in regard to consumption and production. We have seen this already in regard to decisions involving particular forms of indiscriminate benefit where the choices of the minority are necessarily overruled. It is now necessary to recognise that beyond these it involves decisions affecting the entire framework of law and administrative action within which all other acts of choice have to function. That is to say – and it cannot be said too emphatically – that *it involves a liberty to destroy liberty*, to enforce an obliteration of individual choice over the wide field in which individual choice would be

---

*F. A. Hayek, *The Constitution of Liberty* (Chicago University Press, 1960).

†That is to say ignoring definitions which confuse the issue by extending it to cover absence of scarcity, minimum standards of life *et al*. See my *Politics and Economics*, pp. 93–4.

technically practicable. Thus for the libertarian it presents quite peculiar problems. He may admit – indeed, in my judgement he *should* admit – the right of the individual, where responsibility to others is not involved, to extinguish *his own* liberty by the ultimate act of suicide. But he may legitimately have reservations concerning the right of majorities to impose on minorities what the latter may regard as the extinction of their liberties in circumstances in which no obvious social necessity is at stake. He may well deny the rights of minorities of monarchs or oligarchs to restrict the liberties of the majorities over which they rule. But should he not have some qualms concerning the rights of democratic majorities to restrict the liberties of those who do not happen to agree with them?

No short description would be true of the attitude of the Classical Economists on such questions. In the eighteenth century, although Hume wrote on political subjects and even allowed himself the luxury of an essay on *The Idea of a Perfect Commonwealth*, yet neither he nor Adam Smith concerned themselves very much with the advocacy of change in the then status quo of the government of the United Kingdom, which in those days was perhaps considerably more difficult to classify under any single heading that it is today – perhaps the only simple thing that could be said of it was that it was not an absolute monarchy and it was not yet a democracy. As time went on, however, constitutional reform became a much more widely disputed question. I do not know of any important Classical Economist who was opposed to the Reform Act of 1832 which eliminated the worst anomalies of the oligarchic system. But, beyond that, there were acute differences of opinion among those who in other respects must be regarded as Liberal reformers. There were those, such as Macaulay, Senior and Walter Bagehot, who openly confessed apprehension of further extension of the franchise on the ground that it would lead to the spoilation of the rich by the poor in the – mistaken – belief, on the part of the voters, that this would lead to greatly increased wealth all round. And there were Bentham and his followers (including Ricardo) who were in favour of a universal franchise subject to certain conditions and exceptions.

It is worth dwelling a little on the position of this latter group if we are to understand the very substantial difference between the attitude of these great theorists of democracy and what democracy has become today.

First, there were no exclusions on grounds of sex or race. James Mill, it is true, thought that women were best left out – his own marriage, as we know, was not a very happy one. But both Bentham and John Stuart Mill were positive on this point; indeed the *Subjection of Women* of the latter must be regarded as the finest and most cogent of all pleas for the equal political and legal treatment of the two sexes. And the pseudo-science of race which dates from a later period would certainly have been regarded by all of them as beneath contempt.

They did assume, however, a capacity on the part of the voter to be influenced by reason and persuasion – a capacity defined by John Stuart Mill as ability to read and write and to do simple operations in the rule of three. This assumption quite explicitly excluded those who failed to possess such elementary qualities of literacy and numeracy. Thus they would not have acknowledged the entitlement to vote of the millions, unable to read or write or count beyond their fingers, which is taken for granted in many modern democracies. But, needless to say, in sharp contrast to the practice of modern racialists, they would have regarded it as a duty of the government of such communities to bend every reasonable effort to eliminate this kind of incapacity as soon as practicable and so to remove the disqualification. Although more recent developments are probably irreversible, I personally would support the Classical reservations as regards a minimum educational qualification, just as I would support, equally strongly, the obligation of the state to take all appropriate measures to secure that it is achieved all round.

There was a further reservation in the Classical position which deserves explicit statement. It held very strongly that persons in direct receipt of relief by the state while in that state should not be entitled to vote. The reason for this is clear: those who receive benefits for which others are paying should not participate in the determination of the amount. But there are also considerations which tend the other way. If the occasion for relief is voluntary, in the shape of deliberate unwillingness to work, then the argument for withholding voting rights is pretty convincing. But if it is misfortune –

involuntary unemployment, sickness or old age – the argument for deprivation is less cogent. I mention the problem here, not in order to solve it either way but only to make explicit the logical basis of the Classical attitude and, at the same time, to indicate some vulnerability here to reasonable criticism which, personally, I would not admit in regard to its reservations with respect to literacy.

Such reservations apart, the early Philosophical Radicals seem to have had no further fears regarding majority rule with virtual universal suffrage. Not so John Stuart Mill, whose *Representative Government* is at once an expression of apprehension regarding such a state of affairs and the most powerful state-ment of the arguments for its adoption. Mill's fears were two-fold. On the one hand was an empirical problem: he doubted whether democracy, constituted on these lines, would produce representatives of sufficient quality to provide the necessary leadership. On the other hand a matter of principle: unlimited power on the part of majorities involved the power to suppress minorities, to invade their rights outside those other-regarding activities which afforded in his judgement the one permanent sphere for regulative action on the part of governments. It is difficult nowadays to argue that neither of these fears has been justified. We have sufficient experience of democracy to realise that, though there have been some notable exceptions, it does not necessarily produce leaders whose qualities of intellect or integrity commend themselves to sensitive judgement. The only solid recommendation of democracy, from the utilitarian point of view, is that it allows change of leading personalities without shooting – no inconsiderable advantage. As for the invasion of the rights of minorities, do we not see it around us every day, inspired sometimes by perverse or unreflecting idealism but more frequently by the low-brow passions of envy and in-tolerance of the unusual?

So much scarcely needs demonstration. What to do about it is another question. As regards leadership, I suspect that the most we can do is to go on arguing according to our lights, in the hope, not hitherto often justified, that, in the end, Mill's reason and persuasion may create a public opinion less respon-sive to the specious and the discreditable and more critical of the charlatan. Bernard Shaw's superman is not likely to breed in large numbers and, in any case, he may be difficult to identify: and, as we know, in his dotage his distinguished proponent, who afforded such entertainment and dispelled so much nonsense in earlier days, despairing of contemporary democracy, had touched his hat to nearly every scoundrel in Europe – Stalin, Hitler, Mussolini; and John Stuart Mill's incidental suggestion of plural voting for superior qualifications seems scarcely more attractive or plausible. At any rate half a century in university life has not convinced the present writer that there is a higher percentage of political wisdom among academics than elsewhere in the community.

As for the position and protection of minorities, John Stuart Mill relied chiefly on proportional representation: a device which in different forms has actually been adopted in many modern democracies. In principle there can surely be no answer to his arguments: and I suspect that on the practical plane there is also a balance of advantage in this arrangement. It may tend to a greater degree of confusion of issues than the system of simple majority rule. But it tends also to moderation, the absence of violent swings and a greater degree of continuity in the main lines of policy. All things considered, it is probably better than the alternative. I do not think that its predicted accompaniment, the absence of 'strong' government, is necessarily a disadvantage. Certainly the record of the United Kingdom since the war, with its system of simple majority rule, is not so conspicuously better than that of countries elsewhere which have adopted some form of the other system, as to inspire strong resistance to experiment with such an alternative.

In the final analysis, however, if we approach the problem as we have done here, with the objective of providing the maximum safeguard of liberty in general, such devices are not sufficient. It is probable that there is no ultimate solution of this problem under any form of government – our criticisms of modern democracy do not imply that monarchical or oligarchic regimes in this respect were necessarily any better. The most that we can hope for is a brake on precipitate decisions. With single-chamber government, often justified by appeals to the requirements of democratic theory, this is lacking, either with or without proportional representation. A much greater safeguard is provided by the device of a written constitution, interpreted by an independent judiciary, and capable only of alteration after a period of delay with the assent of stipulated proportions of the electorate appreciably higher than mere majorities. There can be no doubt that such arrangements tend to slower rates of change than slap-dash decisions of precariously based, but legally completely sovereign governments. But in regard to the major functions which they exist to serve, at any rate in the domestic sphere, this is seldom a disadvantage. The safeguard of a pause and judicial review of consistency with the fundamental liberties more than outweighs the alleged inconveniences of relative inflexibility. The only sphere in which the government of the United States, for example, is at a real disadvantage, compared with governments less restrained by orderly arrangements, is in respect of foreign policy. It is doubtful, however, whether this is an inherent, rather than an incidental, property of written constitutions and the division of powers in general. But, whether that is so or not, the coexistence in the world we inhabit of separate states gives rise to problems which require further investigation, even on the plane of generality on which this chapter is necessarily moving.

INTERNATIONAL RELATIONS

We have examined already the fallacy of the hopes on which the Liberal Theory of International Relations was founded. Ignoring the lessons of the past, which showed unmistakably that disharmonies arising from independent local economic policies were only eliminated when the power to pursue such policies had been taken over by the national authorities, it assumed that the disadvantages of monetary and commercial interventionism on the part of national states had only to be demonstrated by intellectual analysis for the authorities concerned to abstain from such practices. While it would have been contrary to its most basic principles to assume that the System of Economic Freedom could function properly without a framework of law and order *within* states, it assumed, consciously or unconsciously, that it could function without let or hindrance in transaction *between* persons living in different national areas – an assumption more appropriate to Philosophical Anarchism than to Classical Liberalism.

Much worse than this was the entanglement of historic Liberalism with Nationalism and its emphasis on independent sovereignty. Of course, in so far as the support of nationalist movements implied merely support of opposition to discrimination, on religious or racial grounds, as regards voting rights and employment, there was nothing in this incompatible with the fundamental Liberal outlook, indeed very much the contrary. But the remedy for such abuses is their removal, not the creation of new centres of independent governmental initiative, subject to no restraints save those of an intangible so-called international law with no machinery of enforcement. Such creations were indeed conducive to all the tendencies which were inimical to the fundamental Liberal principle; and when combined with the emotive emphasis on differences of language which usually went with them – next to religion the most divisive obstacle to inter-communal understanding – they were a powerful influence tending to the increase of the fateful disunity of Western Civilisation. Needless to say it would be completely lacking in perspective to speak as if the rise of romantic nationalism took place in a world which had hitherto been free from violent conflict; dynastic rivalry, mercantile greed, the hatreds of various theological sects provide a blood-stained background to the greater part of history since the break up of the Roman Empire. But it is legitimate to argue that the rise of nationalism, in many cases an obvious substitute for religious fanaticism, constituted – and still constitutes – a new obstacle to what Classical Liberalism was trying to achieve. In this connection Hamilton's fundamental proposition has never been refuted. He stated that

A man must be far gone in Utopian speculation who can seriously doubt that . . . states should either be wholly disunited, or only united in partial confederacies, the subdivisions into which they might be thrown would have frequent and violent collisions with each other. To presume a want of motives for such contests as an argument against their existence would be to forget that men are ambitious, vindictive and rapacious. To look for a continuation of harmony between a number of independent, unconnected sovereignties situated in the same neighbourhood would be to disregard the uniform course of human events, and to set at defiance, the accumulated experience of ages.*

It follows, therefore, in principle, that the aim of policy should be to extend to the international sphere the essential conditions of orderly freedom already postulated for domestic affairs, namely an apparatus of law backed by coercive sanction and appropriate judical review. This does not mean that all the functions of government should be centralised; at the present day there is much to be done by way of devolution of many administrative functions, even within existing national states; and it would clearly be a grave impediment to the efficiency of any federal or confederal authority to attempt to assume all the powers hitherto discharged by national authorities. But it does mean that *where the existence of independent powers of initiative, both in spheres of defence and foreign relations and certain spheres of economic initiative, the maintenance of a unit of account for instance and the regulation of inter-local trade and financial relations, is inimical to international order and freedom, these should be assumed by an appropriately constituted central authority.* It does not mean that where differences of language and religion persist, they should be obliterated by illiberal restrictions. But it does mean that they should not be allowed to provide a mystical basis for an independence of states destructive of peace and the civilised intercourse of law-abiding citizens. A liberal will rejoice at the variety of human affairs. But he will deplore and oppose by all means at his disposal anything which threatens the authority which makes orderly variety possible.

So much by way of general principle. But clearly, for its realisation a certain minimum degree of like-mindedness is essential: and it does not need very great powers of practical judgement to perceive, in a world so divided as ours, both by rival ideologies and unequal rates of population increase, that where these influences persist, notwithstanding the truly appalling probable consequences of conflict between the major powers, a world federation on the lines indicated above is not

---

* *The Federalist Papers* (London: Mentor, 1961) p. 54.

possible. Whatever may be possible in the future, if and when the fires of the new religion of Communism have burnt themselves out and the dismaying demographic tendencies of many under-developed areas have been arrested, in our time the most that can be hoped for is the preservation of the relatively free civilisations of the West. At its best this would involve the realisation of the dream of Atlantic Union, that is to say some sort of federation of all powers acknowledging the principles of law and freedom which would assume responsibility for defence and the preconditions of stable production and trade. At its minimum it involves some consolidation of the nations of Western Europe in close co-operation with North America in regard to joint interests in the rest of the world.* It is probable that if this is not achieved the days of the free societies are numbered. But here at least the obstacles to achievement are in our hands: there are no technical difficulties which cannot be surmounted if they are tackled seriously. What we need is less disposition to dwell on differences in the past and more vision to perceive present dangers and the future means of overcoming them.

But difficult as this may be, it is clearly not enough. Western Europe and North America are not the whole of 'Western' Civilisation; and if that civilisation is to be preserved, still more if the humane values, of which, despite various historical and present lapses, they are the main custodians, are to extend their influence, it is important that any associations which they may form should be outward-looking and co-operative with others who *truly wish* to co-operate, particularly the other signatories of the North Atlantic Alliance, perhaps itself revised and revivified. I do not believe that the present comprehensive associations, particularly the United Nations, are much better than a dispiriting and expensive farce, unless there is strong and continuing solidarity between the main Western powers within them. But, given such solidarity and given conscious acceptance of the ideals of the Classical social philosophy, I certainly think that we should not despise what moderate progress can be achieved through the less chaotic associations such as GATT, the World Bank, and a reformed International Monetary Fund. I think the world will need something of this

*See p. 167.

sort for more years than it is easy to see ahead: and I think that it will need all the analytical and persuasive powers of the Atlantic Community, both North American and, hopefully, a federation or confederation of Western Europe to make them work for the benefit of mankind.*

THE MENACE TO FREE SOCIETIES

The idea of a free society as presented and discussed in these chapters is nowadays on the defensive both without and within. Externally the seizure of power by determined groups from the weak or corrupt governments of Russia and China, together with the domination by the former, after the Second World War, of important territories in Eastern Europe, has placed large sections of the population of the world under regimes as anti-libertarian as it is possible to imagine, regimes, moreover, which are ceaselessly active, through activities elsewhere and the continued enlargement of the conventional military and naval forces, to bring about further transfers of power. Were it not for the doctrinal quarrels between the hierarchs of these states, as obscure in origin and intellectual content as the disputes between the early Christians reported by Gibbon, the menace to world peace and the free societies would be even greater than it is today – and that is saying much.

But, even internally, the position of the free world is profoundly disquieting. In spite of advances which have raised the condition of its peoples to levels hitherto unprecedented in human history, belief in the system of spontaneous initiative under which they have come about has waned; and with the disturbances involved by unstable money and the growth of power groups inimical to orderly government, men's minds are perplexed. There is an increasing tendency to fly to alleged remedies which frustrate themselves and must eventually lead

---

*In the end so far as Europe is concerned, it is probable that this involves a common money as well as free movement for trade and capital; otherwise divisive influences would persist. But, in present circumstances, this may take time; but if it were achieved the exchange rate of this money *vis-à-vis* the dollar and so on might remain free to move within commonly agreed limits without the world coming to an end. But we should never forget that the absence of a common money, far from conforming to the libertarian ideal, almost certainly involves a proliferation of controls which is contrary to it. See above pp. 162–3.

to the extinction of liberty itself. The Atlantic Alliance which has hitherto kept the totalitarian menace at bay, is perceptibly weakening from lack of willingness to make the sacrifices which are necessary to keep it strong.

> Things fall apart. The centre will not hold.
> Mere anarchy is loosed upon the world. . . .
> The best lack all conviction while the worst
> Are filled with passionate intensity.

Thus in moments of despondency, one is tempted to think that what has been achieved so far in the elimination of arbitrary power and the creation of a humane civilisation may give way to the unfreedom and intolerance which hitherto, with few exceptions, has been the lot of the major part of mankind, made much worse nowadays by the uniformity of subjection which modern methods of espionage and modern military weapons make it possible to enforce.

This may indeed be our fate. But it is not inevitable. The mass manifestations are dismaying, myopic nationalism; disintegrating international order and, within national areas, the growth of Syndicalistic powers – even inimical to moderate Collectivism; the lack of respect for law; a self-stultifying egalitarianism, based on envy or unreflecting sentiment, which, rather than aiming at equality of opportunity – a noble objective – aims instead at a dead levelling of excellence and its reward; perhaps, above all, the prevalence of a belief, based upon the undoubted achievements of science and fostered by popular writers on economics, that the age of scarcity is at an end and that only ignorance or sinister interest prevent the attainment for all of the standards of opulence presented by popular novelists and the media, magnified out of all statistical proportion to the actual facts of the situation.

These are formidable influences, as we know too well, presenting the maximum opportunity for the specious oratory of the demagogue and the ceaseless machination of the deliberate enemies of freedom. But against these must be set the fact of growing capacity for rational apprehension and reasoning on the part of the individual citizen. The fanatics and the self-seekers in public life are a terrifying spectacle nowadays. But they exemplify a lower order of morality and intelligence than that of many of those they are supposed to represent. There is probably now, among the citizens of contemporary democracies, more kindliness, more tolerance, more decency and – what is peculiarly relevant in the situation we are discussing – more capacity to comprehend the facts of relatively complicated situations, when they are candidly explained, than ever before. After all the age which has seen the consolidation of restrictive practices and the menace to the freedom of the Press has also seen the emancipation of women and the creation of educational opportunities for all.

There is therefore no occasion to despair. Although the brute forces which have been aroused by mass propaganda and appeal to short-period self-interest seem at times to be almost irresistible and the dawn of a new dark age to be at hand, it is difficult to believe that, if they could be made to realise what is happening, the majority of ordinary people would willingly prefer policies which lead to social chaos and the abrogation of liberty. In the short run the advantage is all with the opponents of the free society. 'Bad talk tends to drive out good', as Frank Knight used to say. But in the long run there is at least a chance that more sensible views may prevail. At any rate, to proceed on this assumption is the only course consistent with the duty and self-respect of those who still believe in civilised standards. Better to go down fighting than to compromise with the substitute religions and the sentimental velleities which today threaten the existence of so much which has been so hardly won by the intellectual fathers that begat us.

Index

accumulation: some necessarily governed by collective decision 26; under twentieth-century Communism practised to severe disadvantage of standards of living of mass of the people 26–7; no convincing justification for limitation of private choice as regards disposal of income net of tax 27; an essential assumption of Classical hopes for 'improvement' 106; limited belief in such benefits by Malthus, Lauderdale and their followers 25, 33, 106

advertisement: a leading species of the larger genus, information combined with persuasion 17; effects capable of considerable exaggeration 17–18; desirability of control in certain connections 18

aggregate expenditure: principles of control 97–8; control not a cure-all 99

allocation under Collectivism: not subject of serious attention until twentieth century 143; the problem posed by von Mises 143; attempted solutions of Lange and Lerner 143–4; von Mises's position weakened by overstatement 144; practicable in a war economy 144; with more varied objectives has tendency to run into just such difficulties as suggested by von Mises 144–5; experience of Iron Curtain countries cited 145

assumption of tendency to reasonably full employment, not self-evident 63–4; discussion side-tracked in Classical period by controversy relating to so-called Law of Markets 64–8; resolution of the problem by John Stuart Mill 66–7

Atlantic Alliance (or Union): desirability that it should be outward looking 189–90

Attwood, Thomas: his insight into causes of post Napoleonic Depression superior to that of Classical orthodoxy 72–3; his *Letters to the Earl of Liverpool* quoted 72–3n.

Babour, David: his *Theory of Bimetallism* cited 74

Bacon, Francis: on desirable diffusion of property 111

Bagehot, Walter: his formulation of the duties of a Central Bank 78–9; his apprehensions of extension of the franchise 182

Bank Act of 1844: the controversy regarding its effectiveness 78

bank rate: as traditional instrument of policy 88; virtual cessation of belief in its utility during the 1930s and 1940s 88–9; illustrated by surprising declaration of Treasury official 89n.; revival of some belief in use in early 1950s 90

Banking School: its position in regard to convertibility and reserves 76–7; on the relation between prices and the circulation 77

Barone, Enrico: his alleged solution of the problem of allocation under Collectivism 143; his geometrical illustration of the *Theory of Comparative Costs* 155 n.

193

Index

Ellis, William: a populariser of
Classical theory regarding benefits
of invention 104
employment: desirability of high levels
of, a concept going back to Petty and
not at all ignored by Classical
Economists 86
employment policy: preoccupation
with promoted by inter-war
depression and fear of post-war
slump 84–5; its ambiguities as
regards measurement and relation
to demands for pay 85–8;
Coalition White Paper avoids term
'full employment' 86; insistence
on due regard to avoidance of
inflation does not preclude
prevention of unemployment due
to positive deflation 97–8
equality of opportunity: a desirable
objective to be sharply distinguished
from enforced equality of eventual
reward 109–10
estate duties *versus* legacy duties: the
author's strong preference for
latter 117–18
European Union: a prime *desideratum*
both for absence of obstacles to
economic co-operation and effective
defence against piecemeal invasion
189; its insufficiency without close
alliance with other Western powers
189
evolution of company law and formal
regulation preferable to direct
control 46
external diseconomies of consumption:
exemplified by pollution and noise
19; wider aspects of problem in
connection with general lay-out of
the environment 19–20; neglect
of this problem by Classical
Economists 20; extensive damage
to environment in England largely a
twentieth-century development 20;
danger of concept being used as
excuse for excessive paternalism 21
external diseconomies of production:
parallel to diseconomies of consumption but more recognised by
Classical Economists 38–9; many
remediable by control, some however
aspects of population problem 39

external economies of production: the
argument for protection of infant
industries, its formal validity
admitted though not necessarily
practical application 40–1; its
extension to 'invalid' industries
much more dubious 41–2

Fabian outlook: its tendency to regard
all productive activities as similar
to so-called 'public utilities' 54, 136
fiscal policy: in regard to over-all
stabilisation 88–90; its uses and
possible dangers 99
floating exchange rates: as means of
international equilibration 160–1;
complete freedom unlikely 161–2;
a condition involving persistent abrogation of freedom of contract 163
free societies: present dangers from
without and within 190–2
freedom: interference with on grounds
of differences of taste deprecated
22; as an end and as a means 28
Friedman, Milton: his *Monetary
History of the United States* cited 89;
the author's agreement with his
insistence that control of increase of
money an essential *desideratum* 98;
reservations regarding self-denying
ordinance as regards use of fiscal
policy 99
'full employment': does not mean
zero unemployment 86–7;
irrationality of pursuit regardless of
tendencies to inflation 87
Fullerton, John: a member of the
Banking School 76
Furness, Edgar: his *Position of the
Labourer in a System of Nationalism*
cited as evidence of 'defence of
subsistence wages' in pre-Classical
days 102

giant photographs and a popular
shrine: their part in conditioning
opinion in the Soviet Union 146
Gibbon: the disputes between the
Soviet Union and China compared
to his record of the doctrinal
controversies between the early
Christian sects 190

Index